THE GREAT
Brain
BOOK

AN INSIDE LOOK AT
THE INSIDE OF YOUR HEAD

HP NEWQUIST

ILLUSTRATIONS BY KEITH KASNOT AND E

Library of Congress Cataloging-in-Publication Data
Newquist, H. P. (Harvey P.)
The great brain book/by Harvey Newquist.
160p.   22x27cm
Includes bibliographical references.
ISBN 0-439-45895-1 (alk. paper)
1. Brain—Juvenile literature.   I. Title.
QP361.5.N49 2005
612.8'2—dc22   2004042955

10 9 8 7 6 5 4 3 2 1   05 06 07 08
Printed in China   First printing, March 2005

 Photo Credits

Front cover: © Digital Art/CORBIS
Back jacket: © CORBIS
Page 14: © Douglas P. Wilson/Frank Lene Picture Agency/CORBIS; page 17: © Edward S. Ross/Phototake, NY, NY; page 19: © Douglas P. Wilson/Frank Lene Picture Agency/CORBIS; page 22: © Getty Images; page 24: © Stapelton Collection/CORBIS; page 25: © AP/Wide World Photos, NY, NY; page 26: © The Granger Collection, NY, NY; page 28: © Archivo Iconografico, S.A./CORBIS; page 30: © Bettmann/CORBIS; page 31: © Bettmann/CORBIS; page 34: © H. Damasio, University of Iowa College of Medicine; page 35: © Woburn Public Library, Woburn, MA; page 38: © Getty Images; page 39: © Massachusetts General Hospital, Archives and Special Collections; page 41: © Keith Kasnot; page 43 (top left): © James Holmes/Photo Researchers; page 43 (center): © Richard T. Nowitz/CORBIS; page 86: © Collection CNRI/Phototake, NY, NY; page 105: © DS ART, Homewood, AL; page 110: © AP/Wide World Photos, NY, NY; page 116: © Time Life Pictures/Getty Images; page 119: © Staffan Wibstrand/CORBIS; page 122: © Erich Lessing/Art Resource, NY; page 127: © Bettmann/CORBIS; page 130 (left): © Science Photo Library/Photo Researchers; page 130 (right): © Science Photo Library/Photo Researchers; page 131 (left): © Imagestate, NY, NY; page 131 (right): © Science Photo Library/Photo Researchers; page 137: © Science Photo Library/Photo Researchers; page 144: © Stephen Frink/CORBIS; page 151: © Custom Medical Stock Photo, Chicago, IL; page 152: © Time Life Pictures/Getty Images.

Art Director: Nancy Sabato
Interior design: Tatiana Sperhacke
Interior composition: Kevin Callahan and Tatiana Sperhacke

DEDICATION

This book is dedicated to my nieces and nephews: Jessica, Jacqueline, and Alexandra Folger; Clinton and Wyatt Newquist; Connor, Kyle, Reilly, Aiden, Devin, and "CJ" Johnson; Brandon, Ryan, Tyler, and Ashley Newquist; Jordan and Colin Newquist; Todd, Kassi, and Matt Bradley; and Cole and Paul Barranco.

ACKNOWLEDGMENTS

Authors often like to think that they alone are responsible for the creation of a book. The truth is that no book becomes a reality without the help of many other people. I want to thank Ken Wright for his encouragement and perspicacity, and Kate Waters for her caring and diligence. In addition, this book would not be as beautiful as it is, nor as wonderful to read, without the efforts of Nancy Sabato, Tatiana Sperhacke, Danielle Denega, Melinda Weigel, Eric Brace, and Dwayne Howard.

The following people are deserving of incredible thanks. In many cases, this book is as much theirs as it is mine.

Dr. J. Michael McWhorter, who took me into the "cave of truth." His wife, Barbara, and daughter, Waverley Henderson—along with their extended families—for hospitality that outshines even the best resorts.

Doc's partners, Dr. William Brown and Dr. William Bell, and their staff, for throwing me headfirst into the operating rooms of Winston-Salem's Forsyth Medical Center.

Keith Kasnot, the illustrator of *The Great Brain Book,* who was my first choice to create the images you see here. I am grateful that he signed on, and thrilled with what he produced. His pictures make the brain as close to real as it can get.

My father and mother, both of whom have always encouraged my eclectic interests and writing. My brothers and sisters, and their families, who are as supportive as any one could ever hope for.

Personal thanks for ongoing support go to Michael Johnson and family, Tucker Greco and family, the Cemo family, the Carlsons, John Kunkel, Thomas Werge, Lou Dobbs, and co-conspirators and fellow authors Rich Maloof and Pete Prown.

As always, my eternal gratitude to Trini, Madeline, and Katherine, without whom this—and all my endeavors—would just be words on a page. These women provide a spark for my work that makes it all worth it.

contents

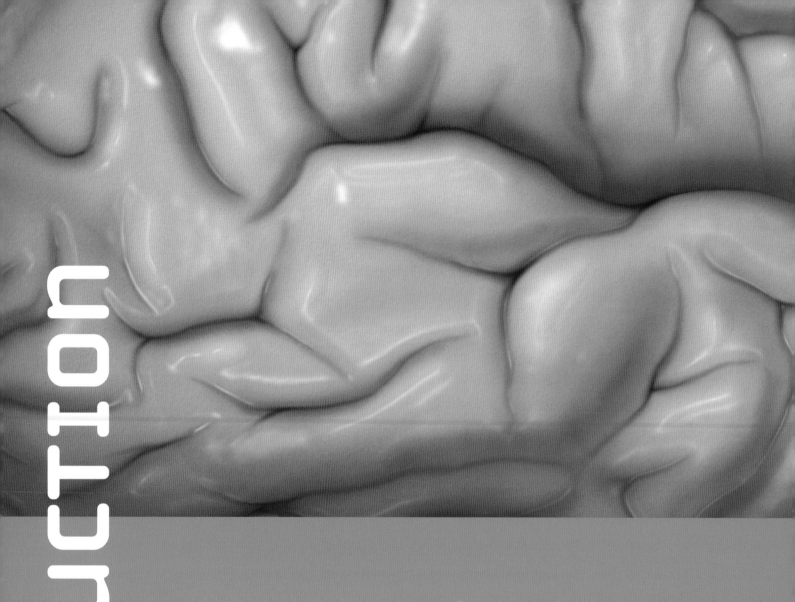

Once upon a time, no one cared about the brain. People used to think that it was little more than stuffing for your head, like straw in a scarecrow. ↗

INTRODUCTION

They thought that all your thinking and all your feelings came from other organs, like your stomach or your lungs.

Over the centuries, scientists and doctors have come to realize that the brain is the most important organ in the body. They discovered that the brain controls everything we do, everything we think, everything we feel, and everything we dream. They realized that the entire body serves the brain.

Studying the brain has not been easy. While you can see how a bicycle moves by looking at the wheels, pedals, and chain, you can't see how your brain works by peeling open a head. The brain works at the microscopic level, and you can't see any moving parts. You can't see how information or pictures or sounds move around inside your head.

Understanding the brain is one of the biggest challenges facing scientists. We're just now beginning to figure out how all the pieces of the brain work, but we have a long way to go. We still don't know how it creates thoughts or how it stores pictures in your head. It's not a photo album or a CD player that just files your favorite images and songs. It's a complicated organ that does billions of things every second that you're alive. That makes it the most powerful organ on earth.

Flip the pages to see what's inside your head!

Introduction

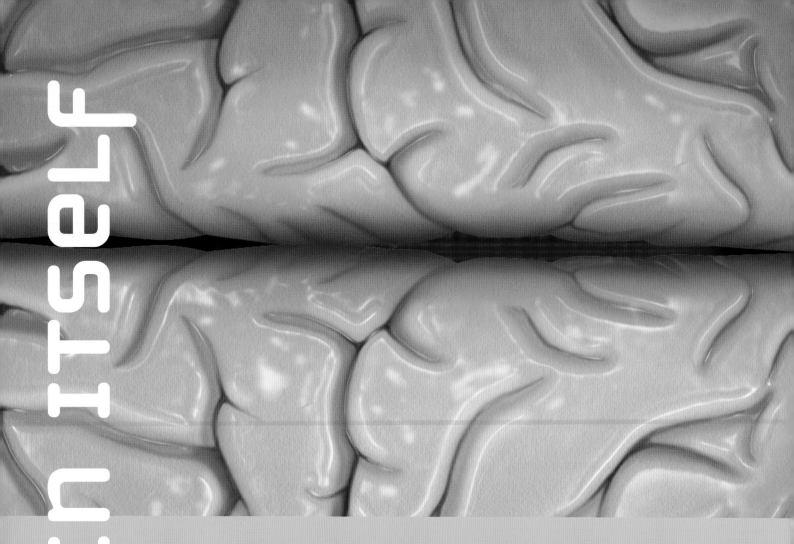

THE BRAIN ITSELF

What is the most complex thing in the universe? Think about it. Could it be a black hole? The rings around Saturn? The space shuttle? A supercomputer? ↗

1 THE BRAIN ITSELF

CHAPTER ONE

It's none of these. The most complicated—and mysterious—thing in the universe is a small organ about the size of a softball. It floats in a solution of clear liquid, is wrapped in thin tissue that looks like it has spiderwebs in it, and has the consistency of a glob of Jell-O. In fact, it is so soft you could easily push your finger into it.

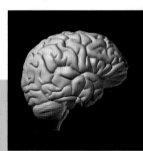

It is your brain.

And even though we use our brains every second of every day, scientists know more about stars exploding billions of light-years away than they do about how the brain does all the things it does.

Why is the brain so mysterious? There are lots of reasons. First, you can't just open up your skull and see how the brain works. It's not like a car with a hood you can open up and watch the engine parts move. If you did open up your skull and mess around with your brain, you could die. Second, all the really interesting activity in the brain occurs at the level of molecules and atoms, which are so small they can hardly be seen, even with the most powerful microscope. Third, we have to use our brains to figure out what our brains do. You can't use a machine to explain the brain—there isn't a computer or robot that's ever been built that knows more than the brain.

You might think that computers would be smarter than our brains. But they can't do many of the simplest things that our brains can do. Here's an example. Lift up your right hand. It's easy to do, isn't it? Yet, this is what your brain had to do just so you could lift your hand: Your eyes had to send the images of the words on this page to your brain. Then your brain had to figure out what those images meant. Once it did that, your brain had to take action. It sent signals down your spinal cord and out to your arm and then down to the muscles in your elbow and hand. In comparison, the most powerful computer in the world can't even read instructions, figure out what they mean, and then follow those instructions.

Let's try something else: Think of a scene from your favorite movie. Sing the song "Happy Birthday" in your head. Imagine a submarine painted yellow. Think of moving just one of your fingers. These are things that you may have done in the past, and you can imagine them from memory.

Now do this: Picture your school's principal wearing angel wings and singing "Happy Birthday." Or picture your principal in a yellow submarine flying through the clouds. You should be able to imagine each of these pretty easily, even though they never really happened. You can "see" and "hear" these images and sounds inside your head. Your brain is so powerful and so creative that it can store images of things you've seen, remember things you've heard, and can even assemble them into scenes you've never experienced before.

But you don't have a camera or a video player or photographs in your head. You have tissue, liquid, nerve cells, chemicals, and blood up there. So where did that image of your principal or the yellow submarine come from? It comes from chemicals and electricity inside your brain. No one knows exactly *how* it all happens, although scientists have some interesting ideas about it.

To show you just how powerful your brain is, take your hands, ball them into fists, and hold them together with your knuckles touching. That's how big your brain is. The one thing scientists do know

This is how big my bRaiN is.

is that your imagination, thoughts, memories, and dreams are created and stored inside a space about as big as your two fists together. You *are* your brain. The brain is capable of creating space shuttles, inventing new machines, writing books, painting pictures, programming computers, playing the piano, making sand castles, reading a magazine, falling in love, getting jealous, feeling angry, and being overwhelmed by sadness or joy. All of these abilities and emotions mix in your brain to make you the kind of person you are.

Your brain controls your entire body. When you think and remember, you are using your brain to do something very specific. At the same time, your brain is also controlling your heart so that blood pumps through your body; it is telling your lungs to breathe; it is determining how often you should blink; it is checking to find out if you are hungry; it is translating the words you're reading on this page so that you understand what they mean; it is listening to the world around you; it is smelling the air. In short, it is doing thousands of things you don't even think about.

Most of us think that when we learn something well, we "can do it without even thinking." This could be jumping rope, riding a scooter, skateboarding, playing the drums, or lots of other things. It may not feel like we're thinking when we do this, but it took our brain a long time to gather all the information on how to do these particular activities. It is stored so well that the brain simply sends the messages straight to our bodies, skipping the whole process where we have to concentrate and feel like we're "thinking." We don't realize how busy our brain is because it does these things almost automatically.

You might think that being able to play baseball or football or soccer is a matter of your body being strong or quick. Strength and quickness are certainly important parts of sports, but the brain is the instrument that makes this possible. For example, the movements that make you a good athlete—throwing a ball straight to a target, dodging another player, running your fastest—are all buried in your brain, which retrieves what you've learned about a sport

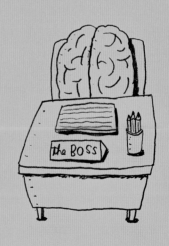

The Brain Itself

and tells your body what to do. If it weren't for your brain, your body would just lie there, unable to run, throw, jump, skip, or even stand.

Human brains have developed two incredibly important abilities that make us completely different from other animals. One is the ability to think. This means we can take in information about the world around us and make decisions about how we want to act. Most animals cannot do this; their actions are based purely on instinct—a natural preprogrammed way to respond to situations. Lions don't choose to hunt; they are born with the need to hunt. Ducks live near water not because they choose to, but because they are born with the knowledge that their food lives in the water. They also know that it is harder for predators to hunt them in the water.

But when humans choose to live somewhere or choose to eat something, we make a conscious decision to do it. We can also make a conscious decision *not* to do it. We have some instincts, but our thinking brains can overrule them. Animals' brains can't do that.

The second thing our brain developed was a sense of "self." We understand that we are unique individuals, different from all the other people around us. We know that we are alive, and that we will die. We understand the consequences of our actions. We know we can choose to do good or bad.

Animals can't do this. They have no concept of living or dying. They don't think about what tomorrow is going to be like, or what they want to be when they grow up. Animals don't think about the difference between good and bad—they just do what their instincts tell them to do.

Of course, animals can be trained to do some things that aren't instinctive. These are usually tricks or types of games. An animal usually learns these tricks by getting food as a reward. One of an animal's most important instincts is to get food, so even teaching it a trick takes advantage of its instincts.

No matter how hard you try, you can't teach an animal to understand and say its name. (A bird, such as a parrot, may be able to say its name, but it doesn't *know* its name.) Animals are limited in what they can communicate. For instance, a dog's bark or a wolf's howl simply serve as warnings, indicate that prey has been caught, or signal hunger or pain. Much of our brain power comes from the ability to create language: to speak, to write, to draw pictures, and to understand what we are hearing or reading.

This is not to say that animals' brains can't do incredible things. Some animals can recognize different shapes, develop new strategies for hunting, and, in the case of certain mammals, even understand symbols. It's just that their brains aren't powerful enough to allow them to make decisions about how to live their lives or to think about all the things they can accomplish. That is the spectacular thing about the human brain. And it is this ability of our brain that makes each human so amazing and so unique.

This is a book about your brain. What it is, where it is, and what it does. We'll look at some of the people who discovered how the brain works, and we'll describe how the brain works.

But let's answer one big question first:
Why do you even need a brain?

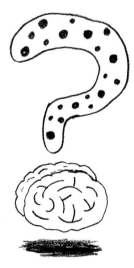

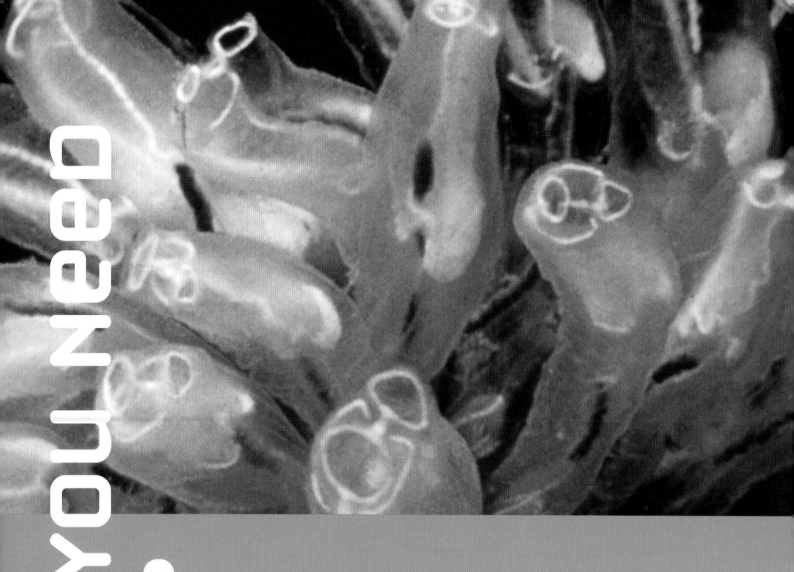

WHY DO YOU NEED A BRAIN?

The brain is the master of all that you do. Every part of your body performs a different job to support the brain. ↗

2 WHY DO YOU NEED A BRAIN?

CHAPTER TWO

Your senses—seeing, hearing, smelling, tasting, and touching—provide the brain with information. Your organs, such as your heart and lungs, provide the blood, oxygen, and nutrients your brain needs to stay healthy.

All creatures that have brains need them for a reason. Brains are how living organisms take in information about the world around them. Brains then act upon that information. Think of the brain as a machine that lets information come in, and also sends out information—like a computer. It receives information, called data, from all of the senses. That's the input, just like when you type information into a computer. Once inside your head, the brain compares it—whenever possible—with data already stored in its memory. The brain makes a decision based on this new information. Then it sends out messages to the rest of the body—the output.

This happens during every event or occurrence in a creature's life. In fact, it's usually happening every single moment that a creature, especially a person, is awake. It might be something as simple as deciding to step over a puddle, or as complicated as learning to drive a car.

Every time the brain gets important information from the senses, it sends out a command to the body to do something about that information. If you are walking up a steep hill, for example, your brain might decide to take an easier route so as not to wear out your body. So it tells the legs to head in a new direction. Or, a hungry stomach may tell your brain that it's time to eat. In ancient times, the brain would have responded to this hunger command by sending your body to go out and hunt for food. Today, it sends your body to the refrigerator.

THE FIRST BRAINS

Hundreds of millions of years ago, even before the dinosaurs, the earliest-known creatures didn't need brains. They just floated in ponds and sucked in little bits of plant life that passed their way. They didn't go looking for their food; it came to them. Over time, many of these creatures evolved to the point that they could choose to move, even if that meant just swimming from one end of their prehistoric pond to the other.

Eventually, these creatures developed small clumps of nerves that allowed them to use this new ability to move. These nerves were bundled together in the area where their senses were located—namely, behind or near their eyes and noses. This bundle of nerves was close to the sensory organs so that data from these organs traveled the shortest possible distance in the creature's body. Now the creatures could actually search for food and avoid other creatures that could also swim and eat *them*.

But the more these little creatures could move, the more information they needed about their environment. They had to consider such things as: Does a particular smell mean food? Is that creature up ahead a possible source of food? Could it be a predator? From what direction is that predator coming? How fast is it coming? That was a lot of data for these tiny creatures to take in, especially those that barely had a brain. All they had to process this information were sensory nerves clumped together that alerted them to the world around them.

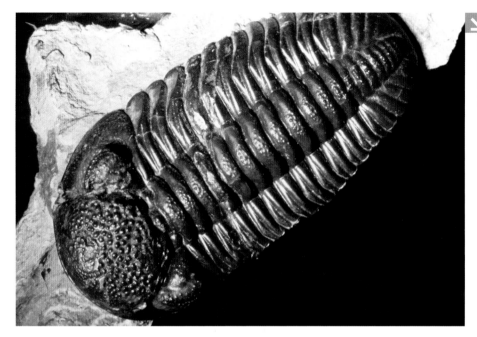

Once upon a time, the trilobite was the most complex form of life on Earth. No brain required.

Over millions of years, this bundle of nerves got bigger and bigger and formed the basis of the brain. More advanced creatures—especially humans—needed a brain because they had to use all their senses to survive. For example, trying to get across a busy street involves sight and sound; walking up steep steps involves touch and sight. If you smell smoke, you'll need to find out if something is on fire, and that involves hearing, seeing, tasting, and smelling. Using all these senses as inputs, the brain makes decisions and tells the body how to act—with caution or quickness, or to fight or to flee.

All this occurs because the brain is the mastermind of the central nervous system (CNS). The CNS includes the three main parts of the brain—the cerebrum, the cerebellum, and the brain stem—and the spinal cord. The spinal cord is a long column of nerves that runs up your back, through your neck, into your brain. It connects the brain to the rest of the body, like the cables that attach a printer, scanner, monitor, and CD burner to your computer.

If we didn't move around or react to our environments, however, we wouldn't need brains. Plants don't need brains because they never move from one place to another. Parts of a plant may move,

The brain and the spinal cord control all the parts of your body in the same way that a computer controls a network of hardware devices.

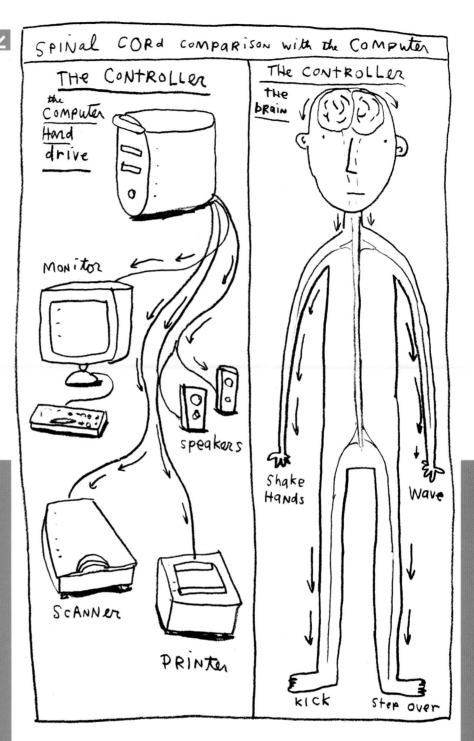

such as leaves and roots. But those movements are reactions to sunlight and the availability of water. They don't make a conscious effort to grow or move. Since plants can't decide to move, a brain would be useless—it would take up unnecessary space.

A creature that eats its own brain? No, it's not a science fiction monster; it's a sea squirt.

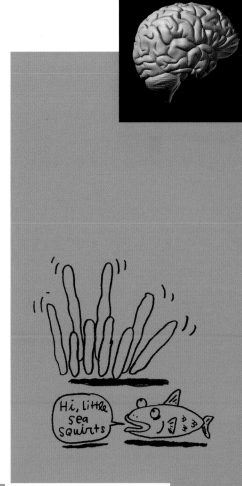

One of the best examples of a creature not needing a brain is the sea squirt. A very primitive form of ocean creature, the sea squirt—which resembles a tadpole—has a tiny knot of nerves that acts as a brain. When it is very young, the sea squirt swims about in the ocean until it finds an object that is stationary, like a rock or a chunk of coral. Then the sea squirt attaches itself to that object—forever. The sea squirt won't ever move again.

From that moment on, the sea squirt collects its food from the water that swirls around it. Since it doesn't move, its primitive little brain is just taking up space that could be used for something else, like collecting or digesting food. So the sea squirt's body begins to dissolve the brain. Some people say that the sea squirt is "eating its own brain." Getting rid of the brain frees up room in the body for more feeding space.

The brainless sea squirt never misses its brain. It spends the rest of its life moving gently back and forth in the ocean currents, appearing to wave to anyone who sees it. For this reason, colonies of sea squirts are known as "dead man's fingers." Some people eat sea squirts as a very fancy type of food, called a delicacy, but I don't think you could call them "brain food."

Why Do You Need a Brain?

Unlike the sea squirt, animals that move around do have brains. To start, let's consider where your brain is right now: It's inside your head. There's a reason it's not in your leg or your wrist or your rib cage. Brains are inside a head because a head is usually in the far front part of a creature's body (as in dogs or lions) or way up top (as in giraffes or deer). For people, it's a little bit of both—up top and a bit out in front. And most sensory organs are in or near the head.

Animals mostly move forward throughout their lives: forward to find food, forward to get from one place to the next (animals rarely move backward unless they're afraid). Moving forward is easy because most sense organs are in the front of the body—eyes, nose, and mouth in front, with ears tilted forward, and hands and feet that move more easily to the front than the back. And since most animals, especially four-legged ones, have a head in the front of the body, it was a natural course of evolution for brains and sense organs to be up front and center.

The position of the head means that the animal or person has a better view of the world and can get as much information as possible. Giraffes can see faraway predators and look for leaves way up in trees, while lions can poke their heads gently through tall grass to sniff out and listen for their prey. Heads are the best places from which to see, hear, and smell the world. And the brain needs to be as close to the action as possible, so that it can make decisions as fast as possible.

Interestingly, it's believed that some dinosaurs—like the stegosaurus—had one brain in their heads and another brain positioned down toward their back legs. The reason for a second brain may have been that the main brain of these huge dinosaurs was only about the size of an orange, which didn't exactly make them the smartest creatures in the world. The second brain—which was most likely a huge bundle of nerves—probably helped the stegosaurus coordinate its legs and its swinging tail. It may have been like needing to have one brain for walking and one brain for chewing gum, so that you could walk and chew gum at the same time.

Your head contains your brain and most of your sensory organs. The brain and sense organs all fit neatly in your skull and need to be protected. The skull is so important that it is often referred to as the "brain box." When you open up the box, there's the brain. We'll take a look at what's inside this box in a while. First, we're going to take a look at how people discovered the brain.

But be prepared. We have to start by going in through the nose.

A HISTORY OF THAT THING INSIDE YOUR HEAD

The brain has been a mystery for as long as people have been interested in the human body. But for much of human history, the brain was thought of as just unimportant goop inside the head. ↗

3 A HISTORY OF THAT THING INSIDE YOUR HEAD

CHAPTER THREE

Ancient people thought that other organs, including the stomach and the heart, were more important than the brain. They even believed that our thoughts came from those organs.

THE EGYPTIANS—SCOOPING OUT THE BRAIN 4000–200 BC

The first people to realize that the brain existed were the Egyptians. They were very smart, even if they didn't think they were using their brains. They built the pyramids of Giza and created one of the first forms of paper. And nearly 5,000 years ago, they started making mummies out of their dead rulers.

The process of making a mummy—called mummification—gives us an idea of what the Egyptians thought of the brain. Rulers were mummified because people believed the spirit of the dead ruler would need his or her body in the afterlife, which was the place that Egyptians believed everyone went after death. This is why the Egyptians put gold, boats, and even toys in the tombs of the dead. They believed these items could be used in the afterlife, just as they could on earth.

But the Egyptians didn't want their dead rulers to have rotting bodies in the afterlife. So they developed a way to preserve bodies for hundreds of years. It was a very intricate procedure that is very difficult for us to duplicate today, even with all our modern tools.

The tomb of boy-king Tutankhamen. All of these items were placed in the tomb for the king's use in the afterlife.

In order to make a mummy, the Egyptians removed all the body's internal organs (after the person was dead, of course). This allowed them to dry out the body, pack it with cloth, and rub it with oils that would help to preserve it. Thinking that certain organs might be useful in the afterlife, they removed the lungs, stomach, liver, intestines, and other organs—usually through a single slit in the body—and placed them in sealed jars. The jars were placed near the mummy in the tomb. They thought that the heart was where the person's thoughts were, so the Egyptians left the heart in the body.

But the brain was a different story. It had to be removed so that the head could be dried out. To achieve this, the people responsible for making mummies broke the nose bone by jamming a chisel into the nostrils. This opened a big hole between the inside of the nose and the brain. Then the mummy makers took a long iron hook, which was like a big knitting needle, and shoved it up the nose of the dead person. Using the hooked end, they pulled out pieces of the brain. Remember, brains are mushy and not solid, so they had to keep grabbing soft chunks of it. Anything that couldn't be gotten out by the hook was later scooped out of the skull with a long, thin spoon.

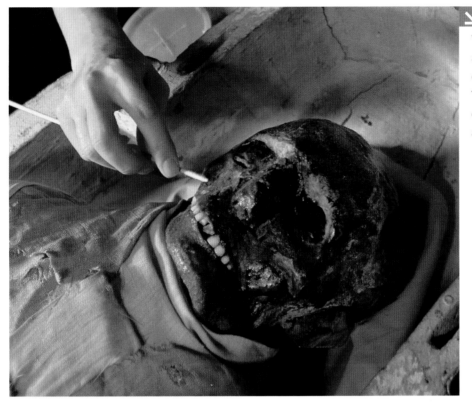

The mummy makers didn't put the pieces of brain in sealed jars. They didn't even put them in the tomb. Instead, they threw away the brain. As far as the Egyptians were concerned, the brain was useless gunk that the dead person wouldn't need in the afterlife.

The Egyptians are famous for the mummies they made, and they learned a lot by cutting open people for mummification. In the process, they became some of history's first doctors and medical scientists. The Egyptians learned a lot about the brain, too, even though they were tossing it out with the garbage.

The first example of anybody anywhere describing the brain is in a document written by Egyptian doctors. The document was written on papyrus, an early type of paper. This particular text was created about 1700 BC (almost four thousand years ago), but it contains information that was probably much older—perhaps from a thousand years earlier. In it, Egyptian doctors describe twenty-seven different head injuries and treatments. More importantly, they discuss the wrinkles and folds in the brain, its outer wrapping, and even the fluid inside it.

A History

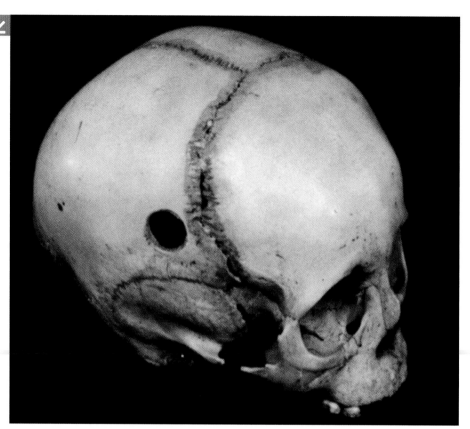

Some ancient cultures believed a hole in the head was good for you. This skull is from the pre-Columbian era. It was found in Peru.

While the Egyptians were scraping the brains out of dead people's heads, people in other parts of the world—especially in South America—were cutting holes in living people's heads. They didn't do this by accident. These "skull holes" were deliberately cut using sharp stone tools and primitive metal blades. Making these holes is called trepanation. No one is quite sure what the purpose was, but we can guess that it might have been to relieve painful headaches, or to help people who had brain diseases. It is also possible that skull holes were made for religious or magical purposes, such as letting spirits into or out of the head.

The problem with cutting a hole in someone's head thousands of years ago was that anesthesia hadn't been invented yet, nor had antibiotics. The people being operated on were probably awake and aware of what was happening. It would be like having someone pound on your head with a screwdriver while you were lying on a couch. The process of trepanation must have been incredibly painful, and a lot of people probably died during the procedure.

A History

THE ANCIENT GREEKS—THE GREAT THINKING BRAINS
500–150 BC

Even though ancient people were viewing and treating the brain, they didn't think the brain had any useful functions. That belief lasted for thousands of years. As late as 350 BC, Aristotle, considered one of the greatest thinkers and philosophers of all time, believed that the center of thought was located in the heart, and that thinking occurred throughout the body. In fact, he believed the brain was the air conditioner that cooled down the heart.

There was a good reason why people believed so many different things about the brain. As far as we know, very few people outside of Egypt, including doctors, had ever examined the inside of a body. Ancient people, as a rule, didn't like cutting bodies open to examine their insides. The human body was considered sacred or holy. After someone died, people in many cultures didn't want a dead person to be cut up because their body was supposed to be returned to the gods or to nature. Even the ancient Greeks—with such advanced thinkers as Aristotle—made laws forbidding experimentation on, and the dissection of, dead bodies.

HEROPHILUS AND GALEN—LOOKING AT THE BODY
AND THE BRAIN (335 BC–AD 200)

A Greek doctor named Herophilus (335–280 BC) got around this law by doing his work in Alexandria, Egypt, which was across the Mediterranean Sea. The rulers of Egypt allowed him to dissect dead bodies (called cadavers) to find out the size, shape, color, hardness, softness, and usefulness of internal organs. These cadavers were usually those of criminals. Herophilus spent a lot of time making detailed observations of the positions of the organs and how they were connected. Because he did so much research, he is known as the father of anatomy.

Herophilus did a very detailed study of the central nervous system, noting that there were different kinds of nerves running to and from the brain. He believed that some nerves controlled movement and

This image of a gladiator and a leopard is part of a mosaic from ancient Rome. Gladiators injured by animals gave doctors plenty of opportunities to look at internal organs, including the brain.

others sent messages. He decided the long-ignored brain was useful after all. Herophilus wrote that thinking occurred in the brain, in the spaces where fluid flowed inside the skull.

While Herophilus was one of the only surgeons of his time officially allowed to see the insides of human bodies, other doctors were determined to learn everything they could. Galen of Pergamon (AD 129–200) was a surgeon who lived in what is now Turkey. He wasn't allowed to do experiments on living humans, but he was in charge of operating on gladiators who were injured in battles. These gladiators suffered some very severe beatings, and Galen was able to look at the insides of their bodies while he tried to patch them up.

Galen also did research on apes and pigs to see if their insides were similar to ours. He eventually came to the conclusion that human brains were extremely important because they not only controlled our thoughts but also contained emotions and stored our memories. He, like many other doctors at that time, believed that our bodies were controlled by four fluids, which were called humors: blood, phlegm, choler, and black bile. Doctors thought that the amount of these fluids in a body determined how healthy or sick a person was. Too much black bile, for instance, made people depressed and unable to eat. Too much yellow bile (choler) made them angry and bad-tempered. While people had believed in the existence of these humors for hundreds of years, Galen was the first to say that our brains actually control us and, therefore, control our thoughts and emotions.

Galen's research was so groundbreaking that most doctors and medical scientists believed his ideas for more than a thousand years. Today, nearly two thousand years later, we realize Galen was on to something—the brain does in fact control our moods. But, as we will see later, it does so by regulating certain chemicals in our body, not by controlling some nonexistent humors.

OUTLINING THE BRAIN—ANDREAS VESALIUS (1514–1564) AND THOMAS WILLIS (1621–1675)

It wasn't until almost fourteen hundred years after Galen's time that doctors started doing significant experiments on the human body. In the 1500s, Andreas Vesalius, a trained artist and a Flemish physician and teacher of anatomy, didn't like relying on the drawings done by Galen and others before him. Those illustrations were old, and Vesalius felt they were incomplete—which was true.

Vesalius wanted to create new drawings, but he needed approval to look inside human bodies. Surprisingly, he was given special permission, but only to work on the cadavers of murderers who had been hanged. He quickly got to work, making notes and drawing pictures as he went along.

In 1543, when he was just twenty-eight years old, Vesalius published his incredibly detailed drawings in a book called *On the Structure of the Human Body*. His training, both as an artist and a doctor, helped him produce the most complete drawings ever made of the inside of the human body. The drawings are so good that medical students still use them today.

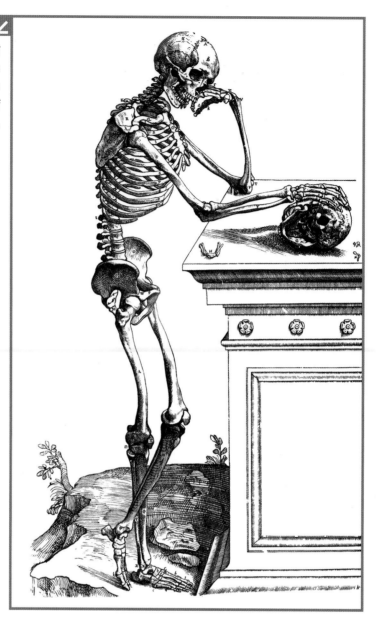

This skeleton looking at another skeleton's skull is on the title page of a book of Vesalius's drawings.

Vesalius studied the brains of animals as well as people. He decided that thinking couldn't happen in the liquid spaces in the brain, as Herophilus had written, because animals had the same kinds of spaces. Therefore, thinking must occur in parts of the brain that were not like animal brains. Like the famous researchers before him, Vesalius was slowly getting closer and closer to the truth of how our brains work.

For the next hundred years, doctors explored the brain in more detail, but had a hard time understanding its functions. Then, in

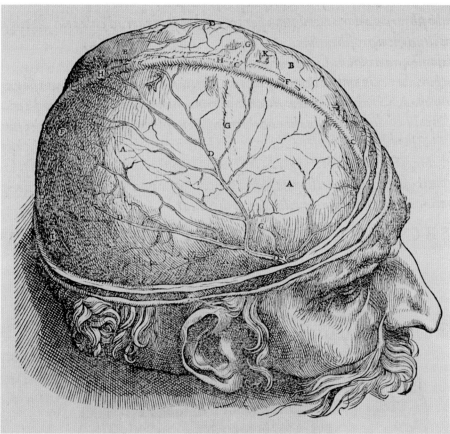

Vesalius's realistic drawings of the brain are still used today.

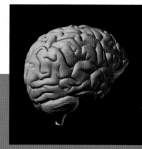

1664, an English doctor named Thomas Willis wrote the first text-book on the brain, describing every part in detail, from nerves to blood vessels. Willis was a renowned professor and doctor at Oxford, one of the world's most important colleges. He was able to dedicate much of his time to studying the brain and all of its parts. He described how different parts of the brain are responsible for different behaviors, such as how the thinking brain is different from the part of the brain that handles functions like walking or breathing. Willis also detailed how blood flows into the brain to keep it healthy.

All of these doctors made great strides in understanding the brain. But their discoveries occurred many years—even centuries—apart. As you'll see, it wasn't until the late 1700s and early 1800s that the study of the brain became one of humankind's most important medical pursuits.

Several events occurred during the 1800s that took brain science further than it had ever gone. These events and discoveries involved three men: Phineas Gage, Paul Broca, and Carl Wernicke. The last two were thrilled to be part of brain history—the first was not.

↘ PHINEAS GAGE—AND THE SPIKE IN BRAIN ACTIVITY

Phineas Gage was a railroad foreman working in Vermont in 1848. It was his job to oversee the crews who cleared out pathways so that new railroad tracks could be laid down. The railroad company considered him a valuable employee and a smart businessman. The people who worked for him respected him as a fair boss and a good man.

One of the most important jobs of the railroad crew was leveling the land and removing huge rocks with explosives. This was done by drilling a hole into the rock, stuffing it with dynamite, and then tamping the dynamite with a long iron rod to make sure the hole was as packed as possible. As the crew boss, it was Phineas's job to do the tamping. The rod he used was 3 feet 7 inches long—a little longer than a yardstick—and weighed 13½ pounds.

On September 13, 1848, Phineas was tamping a hole when the dynamite accidentally exploded right underneath him. The blast shot his tamping iron into the air like a missile. It hit Phineas in the left cheek—and went right through his head. The entire rod came out the top of his skull. Phineas fell bleeding to the ground. His fellow workers screamed; they were sure he'd been killed instantly.

As they rushed over to him, they were shocked to find that Phineas was not dead. Instead, he was wide awake, able to talk, and was trying to get up. Phineas didn't know what happened to him, and acted as though he had only gotten a bad bump on the head.

What had really happened was much more extraordinary. The heavy rod pierced Phineas's left cheek at about the level of his upper teeth. It passed into his skull and shattered his upper jaw, then proceeded upward behind his left eye and directly through his brain. It exited his head by punching a hole almost 4 inches wide through his skull. Two pieces of his broken skull were held in place only by the skin on the top of his head.

Phineas was rushed to a local doctor named John Martyn Harlow. Like the men who worked with Phineas, Dr. Harlow could not believe that Phineas was alive, let alone able to talk. Amazingly, Phineas did not seem to be in that much pain, but Dr. Harlow treated Phineas gingerly. He pushed the two loose skull fragments back into place, and then closed the flap of skin back over the bone. He patched up the hole in Phineas's cheek and then ordered him to bed. Dr. Harlow observed Phineas over the next few weeks, trying to understand how Phineas could have survived an accident that had surely destroyed a part of his brain.

Several months later, after making one of the most remarkable recoveries in medical history, Phineas tried to return to work. He was physically able to do his job, but his behavior had changed— and that was a big problem. He was no longer calm and professional. Instead, he got violently angry and would yell and swear for no reason. He had a hard time making decisions, keeping track of things, and often became confused when doing simple tasks like counting coins. Because he was so difficult to deal with, the railroad company wouldn't hire him back to his old job.

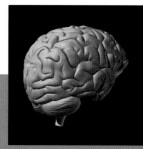

Meanwhile, Dr. Harlow wrote reports on Phineas's accident. Some doctors were intrigued; others didn't believe it. They all wanted to know more. Harlow was invited to speak about Phineas to a group of doctors in Boston. To prove that he was not making up the extraordinary story, Harlow decided to bring Phineas along.

They went to Boston in 1850. Phineas took his tamping iron with him. Indeed, Phineas never went anywhere without it; he kept it with him like a good-luck charm. He sat through Dr. Harlow's presentations and answered doctors' questions. Then he stayed in Boston for several more weeks undergoing examinations by the doctors. Because his wounds had healed, and the skin had covered the openings, some doctors didn't believe the story. After all, he could walk and talk, and he could work. Wouldn't having a hole

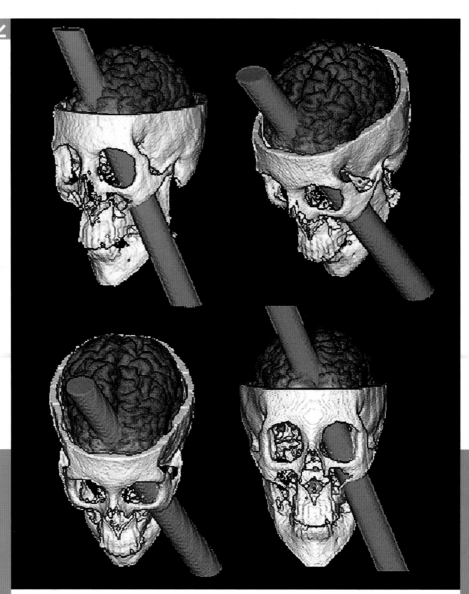

in his brain make him unable to do at least some of these things? He seemed perfectly fine—except for his nastiness.

After the doctors finished examining him, Phineas started traveling around the country. There are reports that he spent time in New York City as part of a museum exhibit and freak show run by P. T. Barnum, who eventually started the Ringling Bros. and Barnum & Bailey Circus. After that, Phineas became a stagecoach driver and took care of horses. Interestingly, it seemed as though Phineas only got along with animals, especially horses. He even went to work on a horse farm in South America.

A History

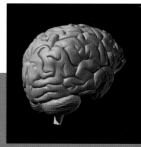

Eventually, the damage to his brain—and his body—caught up with Phineas. His health declined, and in 1859, he went to live with his mother in San Francisco, California. He died on May 21, 1860. For nearly twelve years, he had lived with one of the most incredible injuries in history. When he was buried, his tamping iron was buried with him.

But that is not the end of Phineas's story. Dr. Harlow, who had lost track of Phineas after their visit to Boston, was increasingly curious about why Phineas's personality and behavior had changed so much. By the time Dr. Harlow learned that Phineas had settled in San Francisco, Phineas had been dead for seven years. Still,

A History

Dr. Harlow wanted to examine Phineas's skull to figure out more about what parts of his head and brain had been affected by the accident.

Perhaps knowing that Phineas's case was important to science, Phineas's mother agreed to have his skull brought up out of her son's grave. She sent it, along with the tamping iron, to Dr. Harlow in Massachusetts. In 1868, Dr. Harlow once again presented his research on the change in Phineas's behavior. This time he showed the other doctors exactly how the iron went through Phineas's head, and the damage it caused. This time, they all believed him.

From a closer inspection of the actual damage, medical scientists determined that the front section of Phineas's brain had probably been completely smashed. This led them to believe that the front part of the brain had something to do with how people act in social situations and make sense of the world around them. Phineas's skull and his behavioral changes gave scientists a way to study how a person changed when the front of the brain was damaged.

The bizarre nature of Phineas's injury made him the most studied case in the history of brain science. His skull, along with his precious tamping iron, is still on display in a museum at Harvard University.

PAUL BROCA—FINDING THE KEY IN A MAN NAMED TAN

In April 1861, a little less than a year after Phineas Gage died, a doctor named Paul Broca made an astounding discovery while treating a man called "Tan." He proved once and for all that individual parts of the brain have specific functions.

Broca was a great scientist who studied everything from bones and brains to cartilage and cancer. He was one of the first people to write about ancient peoples cutting holes into living people's skulls.

Broca worked as a surgeon in a Paris hospital. One day, a man named Leborgne was brought to Broca because he had gangrene in his right leg. The strange thing about Leborgne was that he answered every question Broca asked by saying, "Tan! Tan!"

Leborgne seemed to have average intelligence, and he was able to communicate with Broca and the hospital staff using hand gestures. He fed himself, he wandered around, and when he wasn't speaking, he appeared to have no obvious brain problems. Yet no matter what Broca asked him—about his life, about his disease, about what he was thinking—Leborgne always answered "Tan! Tan!" For this reason, everybody in the hospital nicknamed him Tan.

Broca was not able to operate on Tan's leg because Tan died just six days later. Believing that Tan's language problems came from a defect in his brain, Broca decided to have Tan's brain removed for study. Broca examined it right away and found that a part of Tan's brain, on the left side, had been eaten away by disease. Broca figured out that when this part of Tan's brain had dissolved, so had Tan's ability to speak. Without this area, there was no speech.

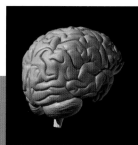

The medical community was amazed by Broca's discovery. Language is a huge part of what differentiates humans from other animals, so locating the precise area of the brain responsible for speech was a huge breakthrough. This section of the brain was eventually named Broca's area in honor of Paul Broca's research.

CARL WERNICKE—TARGETING THE CENTER OF LANGUAGE

Broca's discovery led to lots more research. In 1874, a German doctor named Carl Wernicke went one step beyond Broca. Wernicke was studying patients who—like Tan—had speech problems. Wernicke's patients could speak, but they didn't always make sense. There were times when they couldn't describe what they saw, or they used the wrong words to express themselves. They also had problems comprehending questions. Wernicke determined that something had happened to these people's brains that kept their speech areas from communicating with other brain areas.

X-RAYS

X-rays were discovered in 1895 by Wilhelm Roentgen. Soon after, X-ray pictures were generated in camera-like machines that took pictures of the inside of the human body. They were used primarily to look at solid body parts such as bones. The first time an X-ray machine was used to look at a living person's brain was in 1917. But because the brain is soft and squishy, the X-rays produced only shadowy pictures. X-rays were also limited by their ability to take one picture of one body section at a time, and they couldn't show layers of softer tissue.

However, X-rays did help doctors see problems in the brain. Abnormal growths in the brain, like tumors, show up on X-rays because the growths are denser than the surrounding brain tissue. But X-rays can't help neuroscientists check on how the brain is functioning. Doctors still didn't have any way to see the brain in action.

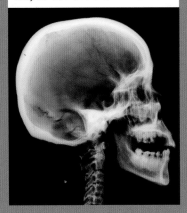

Studying his patients after their deaths, Wernicke found a damaged area in their brains—and it was just behind Broca's area. While Broca's area was the part of the brain that helped people speak, this newly identified area seemed to be responsible for helping people understand language and create sentences that made sense. This language center came to be known as Wernicke's area.

The fact that these two areas were right next to each other, side-by-side in the left half of the brain, opened up a whole new world of brain exploration. In some ways, Broca's and Wernicke's research was among the most important ever done because these two men located two parts of the brain that are responsible for making people different from animals—the ability to create and understand language.

EDUARD HITZIG AND GUSTAV FRITSCH—RIGHT BRAIN CONTROLS LEFT SIDE

From the end of the 1800s into the twentieth century, scientists built on Broca's and Wernicke's work. In 1870, Eduard Hitzig, who was a doctor in the German army, operated on soldiers who had parts of their skulls blown open in battles. Since the brain itself cannot feel pain—we'll find out why later on—Hitzig realized these battlefield injuries were a perfect opportunity to examine the exposed brains in living patients.

Hitzig found that when he touched particular areas of the brain with charged electrical wire, parts of the soldiers' bodies would twitch. He realized that specific areas of the brain must control specific muscles in the arms and legs, like Broca's area controls speech. After the war, Hitzig teamed up with a doctor named Gustav Fritsch, and the two did research on dogs. They found that individual parts of a dog's brain controlled related parts of its body. As they moved the electricity around, they could make any part of the dog twitch, just by touching the correct part of its brain. In this way, Hitzig and Fritsch were able to map out the parts of the brain that controlled movement. Of course, they also found out that some parts of the brain didn't control movement. They

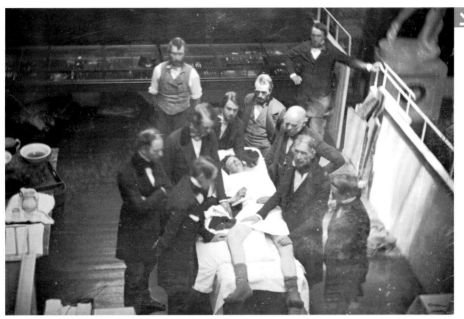

In the nineteenth century and earlier, operating rooms were about as clean as your garage.

thought that these areas probably controlled the senses, such as hearing, seeing, and feeling. And they were right.

Through their experiments, Hitzig and Fritsch also discovered that when they touched the right side of the brain, muscles and limbs on the left side of the body moved. When they touched the left brain, parts on the right side twitched. This was evidence that the left brain controlled the body's right side, and the right brain controlled the left side.

Throughout the nineteenth century, there were more advances in brain science. In Scotland in 1879, a surgeon named William Macewen removed a brain tumor from a patient who had uncontrollable shaking fits, called convulsions. When he examined the patient, Macewen reasoned that the patient's convulsions came from a growth that was damaging the brain. When the time came for the operation, Macewen opened up the patient's skull and found the tumor, just as he had predicted.

(Macewen was a smart guy; he was one of the first surgeons to require that nurses and assistants in his operating room wash their hands before operating on a patient. He also required that surgical tools be sterilized. Before Macewen, dirty scalpels and

ALL Nurses and DocTors must Wash hands before ENtERINg the operating Room.

A History

dirty hands were used to operate on patients. People cleaned up *after* the operation, not before.)

In 1909, building on the work of Broca and Wernicke, German scientist Korbinian Brodmann mapped the cerebral cortex—the wrinkly outside layer of the brain—and identified exactly which brain areas controlled which sensory and motor functions. He assigned a function and a number to forty-seven different areas of the cortex so that researchers could explain to one another which part of the brain they were working on. Up until that point, there were different systems, differing opinions, and incomplete brain maps.

WILDER PENFIELD—THE PERSISTENCE OF MEMORY

During the 1950s, a doctor named Wilder Penfield was working with patients who had epilepsy. Epilepsy is a disorder that causes people to have repeated seizures—or fits—and lose control of their bodies. By touching a patient's brain with a small wire hooked up to a 3-volt battery, Penfield tried to find out which parts of the brain were causing the seizures. He did this while his patients were lying on an operating table. Even though he had removed a part of their skulls, they were fully awake. (He did use anesthesia on their heads so they didn't feel any pain when he opened them up.) Penfield was able to find the source of epileptic seizures—and he also found something much more important.

Penfield discovered that when he touched a wire to different parts of the side of the brain called the temporal lobe, the patients—who were awake—suddenly remembered things from long ago. These memories included the color of their bedroom, a childhood friend, the sound of their dog barking, and so on. Every time he touched the wire to that exact spot, the same memory would come back and the patient would describe it.

As he continued to experiment, he was able to pinpoint areas of the brain that directed movement and controlled the senses. He discovered that the parts of our bodies that are the most sensitive to the outside world—fingers, eyes, mouth—require more working

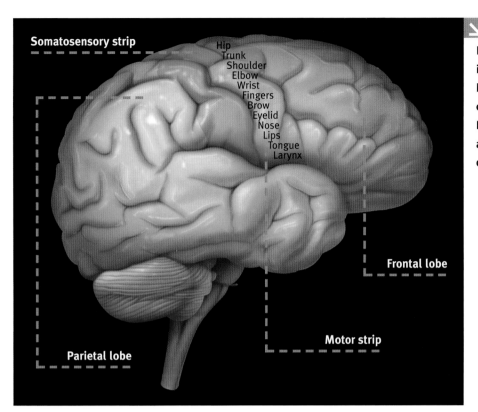

Somatosensory strip

Hip
Trunk
Shoulder
Elbow
Wrist
Fingers
Brow
Eyelid
Nose
Lips
Tongue
Larynx

Frontal lobe

Motor strip

Parietal lobe

Penfield found that individual parts of the brain were in charge of specific body parts. Knee, ankle, and toes are on the other side of the brain.

space in the brain than, say, knees or elbows. The areas of control corresponded to two strips that wrapped around the brain like two imaginary headbands.

The first strip is called the motor strip because each section controls everything that moves in your body, from your eyes to your toes. It runs along the frontal lobe. The second strip, located behind the motor strip on the parietal lobe, is called the somatosensory strip. This is where information is processed about what specific parts of the body are feeling or doing, such as when you touch something and can tell that it is hot or cold. When you press your fingers or toes up against something, the somatosensory strip is where your brain receives this data.

Penfield created a drawing that came to be known as a *homunculus*. A homunculus is a mythical little man, sort of like a troll, with oversized body parts. Penfield's drawing shows what we would look like if our body parts were as big as the brain space they take up. So the homunculus has huge eyes, lips, hands, feet, and a tiny chest, little hips, and small shoulders.

A History

Penfield's research took place half a century ago. Since then, thousands of researchers have pieced together more information about the brain. Using modern tools, they look for clues to how it is constructed and how it works. Almost every day, someone figures out something new that adds to our understanding of the brain.

One of the most fascinating recent discoveries is that almost everything the brain does relies on chemicals called neurotransmitters. These are so small they cannot even be seen with microscopes, yet they affect everything that goes on inside your head—whether you can count to ten, recognize your friend's voice, or are feeling happy or sad. Neurotransmitters are the way cells in the brain communicate with one another and how the brain controls the rest of your body. Brain researchers expect that someday they'll be able to control these neurotransmitters. Finding out more about them may lead to some of the most important scientific discoveries of all time. These discoveries could eventually help patients with a wide variety of medical problems. Diseases such as Parkinson's and disorders such as severe depression may one day be successfully treated by controlling the levels of neurotransmitters.

So, now that we've walked down more than five thousand years of brain history, it's time to look at what all those brain scientists were actually exploring. And since you've got a brain and an imagination, we'll pretend we're putting that brain right here on the table in front of us.

HANS BERGER AND THE EEG

A small section of an EEG report showing brain waves.

Nearly 100 years after it was invented, the EEG is still used to measure brain activity.

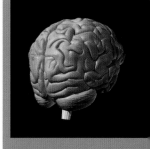

As technology and medical equipment became more advanced in the 1900s, scientists used new devices—usually electrical devices—to explore the brain. A German scientist named Hans Berger believed that if the brain generated electrical activity, it might be possible to measure that activity with an electrical machine—just like you can measure battery power. In 1924, using little stickers called electrodes that were attached to the head, he created an instrument that would detect and record the electrical pulses in the brain, which he called brain waves.

Berger chose an interesting test subject: his fifteen-year-old son, Klaus. Berger found that as Klaus did different things with his brain (such as thinking of math problems or closing his eyes and imagining pictures) different types of electrical activity occurred. Berger discovered that there were normal waves that the brain always generated, and additional waves that were formed when it was doing something unusual or if the brain was damaged. He called his machine an electroencephalograph, or EEG for short. The EEG has become the single most important way to test for healthy brains. It is still used all over the world today.

A History

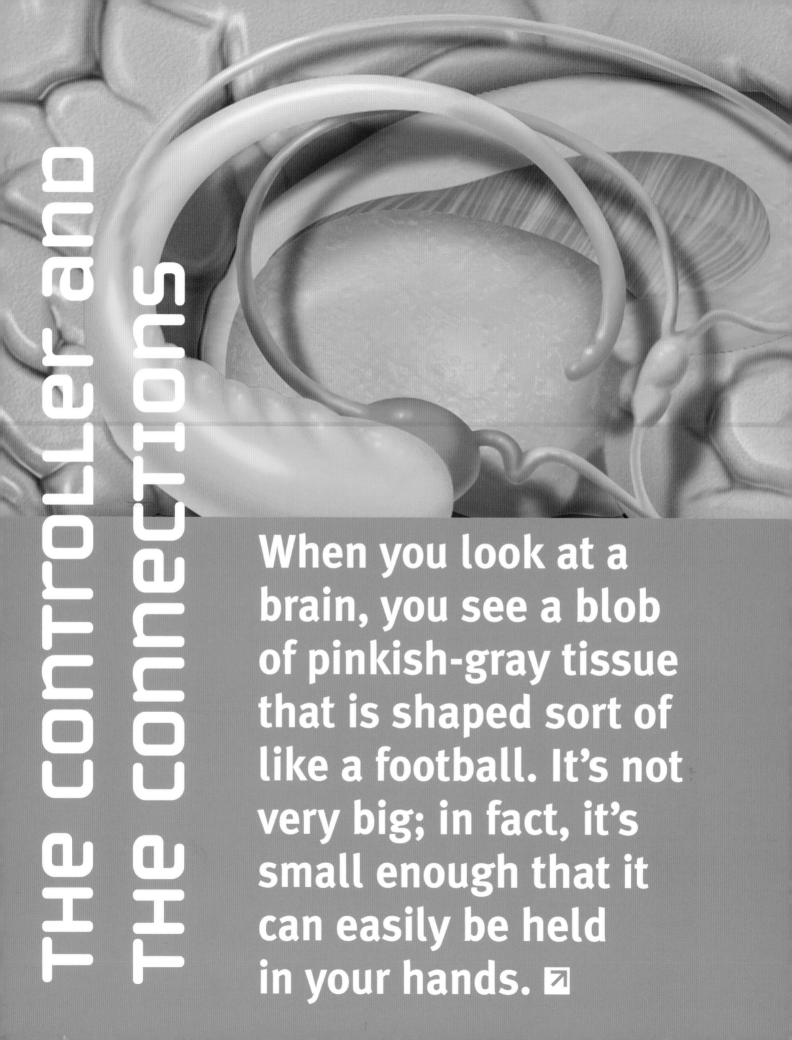

THE CONTROLLER AND THE CONNECTIONS

When you look at a brain, you see a blob of pinkish-gray tissue that is shaped sort of like a football. It's not very big; in fact, it's small enough that it can easily be held in your hands. ↗

4 THE CONTROLLER AND THE CONNECTIONS

CHAPTER FOUR

On the surface, it's a strange-looking organ, like a chunk of coral or a wrinkly rock. There doesn't appear to be too much to it beyond all those wrinkles, but like many things, what's on the inside makes all the difference in the world.

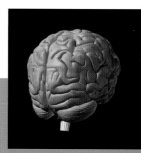

When most people think of the brain, they're thinking of the cerebrum. It's the big wrinkly-looking glob that makes up the largest section of the brain. There are, however, two other important sections. Below the cerebrum, at the base of your skull and above your neck, is the second part, the cerebellum. It sticks out of the back of your cerebrum like a piece of cauliflower. The third part, which runs down from your cerebrum and cerebellum, is the brain stem. This attaches your brain to the rest of your body.

These are the three main parts of the brain. But they are just the sections we can see. The entire brain is made up of many more bits and pieces, like a model airplane or a jigsaw puzzle.

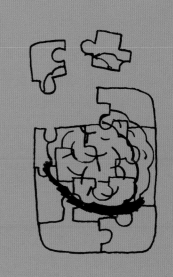

The best way to examine the brain is to split it in two, right down the middle. This gives us two halves, each called a hemisphere. These two hemispheres, the right one and the left one, match each other; they each have identical parts. Once separated, each hemisphere can be divided into four individual chunks, called lobes. The lobes are the frontal (front), temporal (side), parietal (top), and occipital (back).

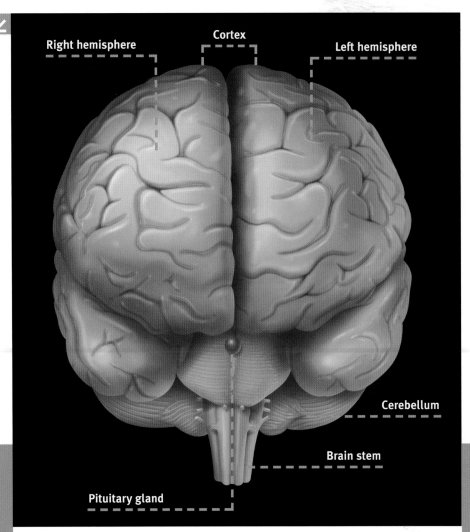

The left and right hemispheres of the brain are almost mirror images of each other.

Right hemisphere

Cortex

Left hemisphere

Cerebellum

Brain stem

Pituitary gland

When you look at the whole brain again, you see that the entire organ is made up of layers, like a cake. The top layer is called the cortex, or gray matter, and it is like the bark of a tree. It covers the entire brain, including the cerebrum and cerebellum. The cortex is called our "thinking brain" because it is where we do our thinking and where our memories are stored. As you'll see, the cortex is the most advanced part of the brain, and its ability to understand language and handle speech is one of the features that differentiates us so much from other creatures.

Beneath the cortex is the white matter. It is made up of billions of microscopic strands of brain cells connected to one another. These cells act like tiny phone wires and are responsible for the brain's communication.

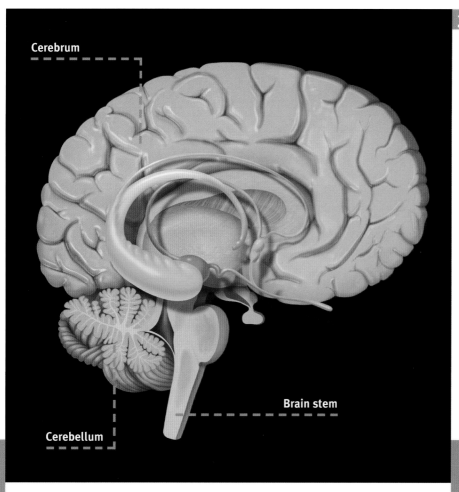

Cerebrum

Cerebellum

Brain stem

This is what the inside of your brain looks like when it's split in half. The limbic system is made up of the parts at the center of this cross section.

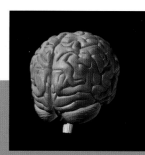

Down below the white matter is the limbic system. This is where your emotions and your feelings are centered. Mammals share some of the same emotions we do, such as fear, and their limbic systems are similar to ours. For this reason, the limbic system is referred to as our "mammalian brain." Tucked beneath the limbic system are structures and glands that control growth, hunger, sleeping cycles, and how we respond to the world around us.

At the base, or bottom, of the brain is the brain stem, which attaches the brain to the rest of the body. Many body functions, especially those we don't think about, are controlled here. These include breathing and the beating of our hearts. The brain stem is called the "reptilian brain" because it is very similar to the brains of such simple creatures as lizards and fish. Their brains don't do much other than keep them alive and help them find food.

The brain stem is called the reptilian brain.

Controller and Connections

This gives you an idea of what we're about to explore. We're going to look at what's called "the big picture" of the brain. That means looking at the whole thing, including its covering, and then examining its individual parts, piece by piece.

THE BRAIN BOX—THE PROTECTIVE COVER

Let's start with your brain's home, the skull—also known as the brain box. "Brain box" is a pretty good description because we're going to open it up and look at everything in there.

Your brain is so fragile that it could easily be splattered into pieces like a mud pie. This is because the brain has nothing in it that is very solid. There is no cartilage or bone that holds it together or binds it into a particular shape. And it isn't made of muscle tissue like the heart, which is tough and holds together tightly.

To ensure its safety, your brain is covered by a thick, hard, bony "box"—your skull. Throughout your life, you'll bump your head countless times—on a swing set, on a playing field, on a door, or against one of your friends. But your skull is thick, and it's thick for one reason: to protect your brain. Other bones in your body, especially your arms and legs, might break when you fall down or smash them against a hard object, but your skull will usually stay intact when you bump it into something. It is difficult to break your skull, but to be on the safe side, a helmet should be worn for certain activities to protect it even more. You can never be too careful when it comes to protecting your brain.

The part of your skull that holds your brain is called the cranium. It is made up of eight major bones, which fit together in a way that makes your head feel solid from front to back. Think of the way pieces snap together in a plastic model, and you'll get the idea. The names of these eight bones correspond to the lobes of the brain: one frontal (front), one occipital (back), two parietals (top), and two temporals (sides). Two additional interior bones, the sphenoid and ethmoid, connect the skull to the face bones. By the way, you have fourteen face bones, and when you add your

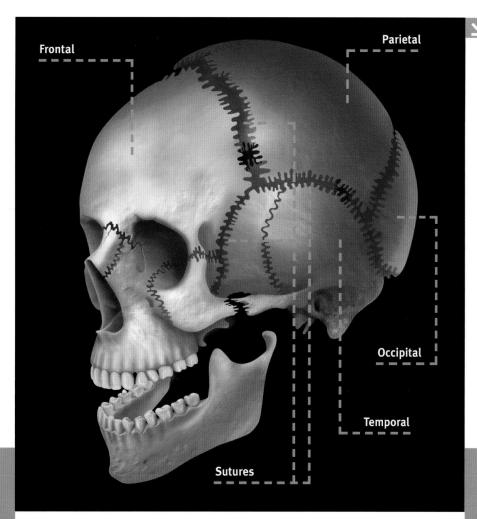

Frontal

Parietal

Occipital

Temporal

Sutures

As you grow, the bones in your skull fuse together to form a solid enclosure for your brain.

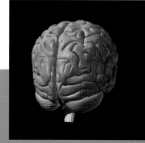

jawbone to this picture, you have a complete skull. Most of what we're interested in, though, happens in the cranium.

The bones of the cranium grow together over time. When a baby is born, you can feel the space between the bones, called sutures, on the baby's skull. The soft spot at the top of the baby's head is where the sutures all meet. That spot eventually closes over, and the cranium is sealed shut like a treasure chest.

The closed skull serves the same purpose as an eggshell, providing cover for the not-so-solid brain inside. At its thickest, the cranium is about 1 centimeter, or a little less than ½ an inch thick. In some areas, it is thinner, about the thickness of a sheet of cardboard. Other than being a protective shell, the skull itself doesn't do much. Think of it as the brain's built-in helmet.

My soft spot feels like an overripe melon.

Controller and Connections

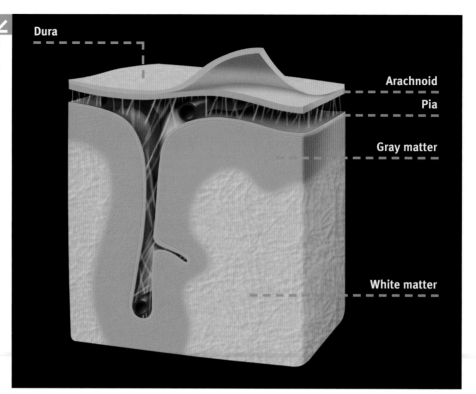

The three layers of the meninges are like protective wrapping paper for the brain. Even the inside of the brain's wrinkles are protected.

Dura

Arachnoid

Pia

Gray matter

White matter

BRAIN SIZE

The average size of an adult brain is about 3 pounds, although there have been some really big ones and really small ones. The smallest human brain ever weighed was 1 pound and belonged to a man named Daniel Lyon. The heaviest was 5 pounds and was supposedly that of a man whose body ended up in a medical laboratory in Ohio. His was almost the weight of two normal brains, yet he had only normal intelligence.

THE MENINGES

When you remove the top of the skull (doctors do it using a small saw called a craniotome), you find that the brain is covered by what looks like leathery wrapping paper. This is called the meninges. It protects the brain the same way you protect something fragile, like when you wrap it in paper, bubble wrap, or newspaper.

The meninges has three layers. The outside layer is called the dura mater. This is tough tissue that keeps the brain attached to the inside of your skull. Underneath that is the arachnoid layer. Notice that the word arachnoid is a lot like "arachnid," which is a word for spider. The arachnoid layer contains a huge number of crisscrossing blood vessels that look like a spiderweb, which is how it got its name. These blood vessels help move blood around the brain and then carry it back into the body where it can be cleaned, filtered, and reused.

The third layer—the one closest to the brain itself—is called the pia mater. It fits snugly around the whole brain—the cerebrum

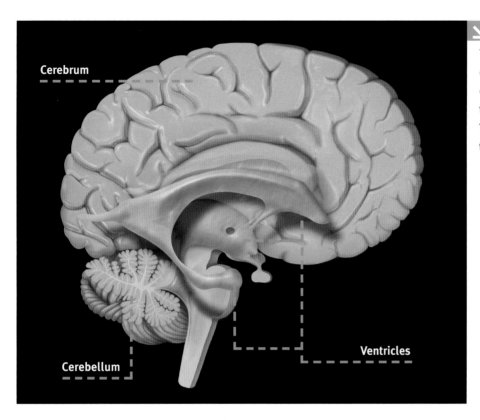

Cerebrum

Cerebellum

Ventricles

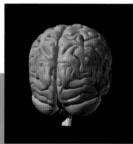

The brain's ventricles contain fluid that both cushions and cleans the inside of your head. The areas in blue are the ventricles.

and the cerebellum—like a piece of plastic shrink-wrap. It even goes down into the wrinkles in the brain. The pia contains some of the blood vessels that supply the two main nutrients the brain needs: glucose and oxygen.

CEREBROSPINAL FLUID

The pia also acts like a protective bag for the brain. There is a thin layer of liquid, called cerebrospinal fluid, between the pia and the arachnoid layer above it. This clear watery fluid takes its name from "cerebro" for cerebrum and "spinal" for the spinal cord, which are the areas that the liquid flows through.

There are only about 5 ounces of cerebrospinal fluid in your entire head—less than half the amount of liquid in a can of soda. But this liquid is important to the brain's safety and health. The cerebrospinal fluid floats around the pia to help cushion the brain inside the skull.

There are also four spaces deep inside the brain that are filled with the same fluid. These spaces are small reservoirs, called ventricles, that function as shock absorbers for the different parts of the brain.

The cerebrospinal fluid serves another function as well: It flushes out the brain, flowing though small spaces and keeping the brain clean by removing any waste products that accumulate, such as dead cells. This waste is then dumped back into the bloodstream via the blood vessels in the arachnoid layer and washed out of the head.

The waste can't get back into the brain because of the pia and something called the blood-brain barrier. These are little blood vessels that are so small that only molecules of oxygen and glucose, which the brain needs, can squeeze through. The blood is delivered to the brain through arteries that snake their way through the brain and into its folds, and then surround it like netting. This blood barrier keeps out anything that the brain can't use or shouldn't be exposed to (such as germs and red blood cells). It's like a water filter: It blocks out all the things the brain doesn't need and lets in the pure stuff.

All these things separate the brain from the outside world. We've got the cranium that surrounds the brain like a sealed box, the layers of meninges that keep it covered like wrapping paper, and the cerebrospinal fluid that keeps it clean and floating.

THE HUMAN BRAIN—THE CEREBRUM

On the surface, the brain is not really much to look at. The inside of a television set might look more interesting. There are no circuits, wires, picture screens, sparks, or electrical flashes in the brain. Instead, it is a rounded lump of wrinkly matter, soft to the touch. Eighty-five percent of the brain is water. Full-grown, it only weighs between 2 and 3 pounds, about the same as a jar of peanut butter.

The most obvious thing about the brain is that it's more wrinkled than your fingers after a day in the pool. These wrinkles form what are called

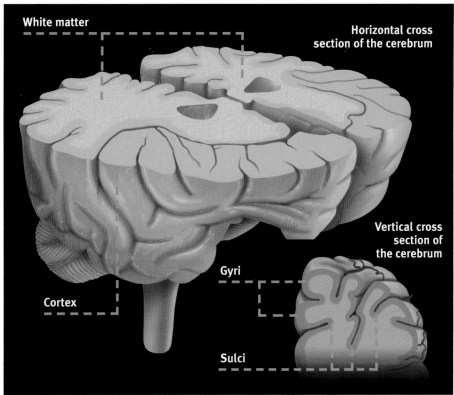

White matter

Horizontal cross section of the cerebrum

Vertical cross section of the cerebrum

Gyri

Cortex

Sulci

This cross section of the brain shows how deep the sulci go.

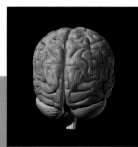

gyri and sulci. The gyri are the folds or hills (a single one is called a gyrus), while the sulci are the grooves or valleys between each fold (one groove is called a sulcus).

Gyri and sulci help identify sections of the brain because they form the division lines between the different lobes. These hills and valleys help scientists determine exactly what part of the brain they're looking at.

There is a reason your brain has so many folds. The folds increase the size of the outside of the brain. To show how this works, take a T-shirt and ball it up. It will be wrinkled, but you can squish it down to a small size. There's still as much T-shirt as there ever was, but you've balled it up nice and tight.

Completely unfolded, the brain would be about 400 square inches, about the size of a pillowcase. But if your brain were flat, then your head would have to be an awful lot bigger. By crinkling it up, you can squish that same amount of material into a much

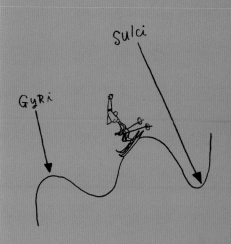

Sulci

Gyri

Controller and Connections

smaller space. The folds in the brain allow it to store more functions and thoughts.

The top layer of the brain's wrinkly surface is called the cortex. The cortex is what most of us picture when we think of the brain. It is about 4 millimeters (⅛ of an inch) deep and is similar to the bark on a tree (the word "cortex" comes from the Latin word for bark). The part of the cortex that covers the cerebrum is the cerebral cortex. The cortex not only covers the surface of the brain but also the space between the hemispheres, so that each hemisphere is covered by its own complete cortex layer. It is often referred to as "gray matter" even though it's really pink when it's inside your head. It's only gray after a brain is dead and all the blood is gone.

Most of the brain is the cerebrum. This is the large soft mushy part that controls most of what is called your "higher," or intelligent, functions, like thinking and speaking. It is split right down the middle and divided into two halves. The two halves, called the left and right hemispheres, are connected by a thin strip of tissue called the corpus callosum. This strip allows the left side of your brain to communicate with the right side of your brain. Why isn't it just one big brain instead of two halves? Well, as Fritsch and Hitzig discovered, the left half of your brain controls the right side of your body, while the right side of your brain controls the left side of your body. It's almost like having two brains—in case one side gets damaged, the other can still perform normally.

⬊ LOBES

Each half of the cerebrum is made up of four sections called lobes. When we talk about lobes, keep in mind that your brain has two of each kind—that makes eight lobes in all. Korbinian Brodmann's map of the brain shows us which lobes are responsible for which functions. It also shows us where certain abilities and behaviors come from. The lobe in the front of the brain is called the frontal lobe. It takes up the space behind your forehead. Next to your ears, tucked just under each parietal lobe, are the temporal lobes—one on each side. The lobe in the back of the

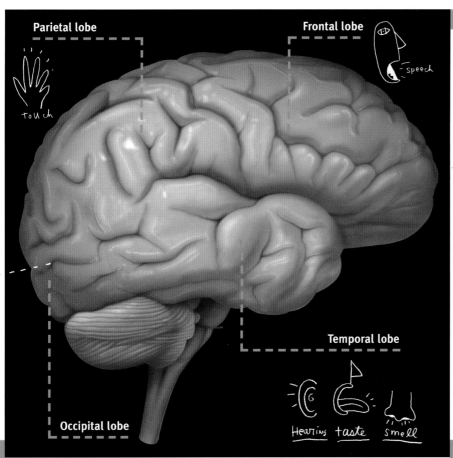

Parietal lobe

touch

Frontal lobe

speech

Temporal lobe

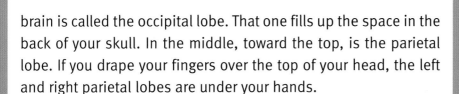

Hearing taste smell

Occipital lobe

The four lobes of the brain—frontal, temporal, occipital, and parietal—handle specific aspects of our bodies and behaviors.

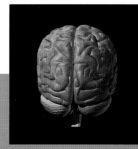

brain is called the occipital lobe. That one fills up the space in the back of your skull. In the middle, toward the top, is the parietal lobe. If you drape your fingers over the top of your head, the left and right parietal lobes are under your hands.

Each pair of lobes has a specific function:
• The frontal lobes control reasoning, memory, and speech.
• The temporal lobes are responsible for hearing, taste, and smell.
• The occipital lobes handle sight and visual information.
• The parietal lobes handle sensory processing, including touch.

Notice that all similar functions are grouped together. The frontal lobe, right where your forehead is, handles many of the functions that make us human, but also make us individuals. It contains our language center, which includes our ability to read, write, and speak. It is the seat of our intelligence, which allows us to think, reason, and make decisions in our daily lives. It also controls our

Controller and Connections

voluntary movements, such as reaching for a glass of water or throwing a ball. Our memories reside in the frontal lobe, and memories contribute to an individual's personality, the kind of person he or she is.

The temporal lobe, right next to your ear, handles the senses of hearing, taste, and smell. There is a direct link from your nose to your temporal lobe called the olfactory tract. When you smell or taste something, the information is processed in the temporal lobe. Memories of flavors, as well as memories of sounds, are also stored in this area for future use.

The occipital lobe, which is at the back of the brain, primarily handles sight information. This information comes from your eyes, which are really an external part of the brain. You might think of eyes as little balls on their own in your face, but they are really an extension of the brain, allowing the brain to look out at the world like a periscope from the safety of your skull. In fact, you don't see with your eyes, you see with your brain. Your eyes just let in the light and the signals that eventually form what you "see" in your brain.

Scientists believe that visual memories are stored in the occipital lobe. When you need to remember how something looks, the frontal lobe—which does your thinking—may call up a visual image from the occipital lobe. It then might call up some sound memories from the temporal lobe and mix them together to create a complete memory. This way, you can remember how someone's voice sounds and how their face looks all at the same time.

The parietal lobe is at the top of your brain, behind your frontal lobe. Much of the information that comes from your senses, especially touch, finds its way here so that your senses and your motor skills can be coordinated. If you smell, see, touch, and taste a hamburger, the parietal lobe is combining that information into one complete package. This area also helps you determine how heavy something is and what its shape and texture are. The parietal lobe is essential for keeping you aware of where your body is relative to other objects, which is known as "spatial awareness." It's what

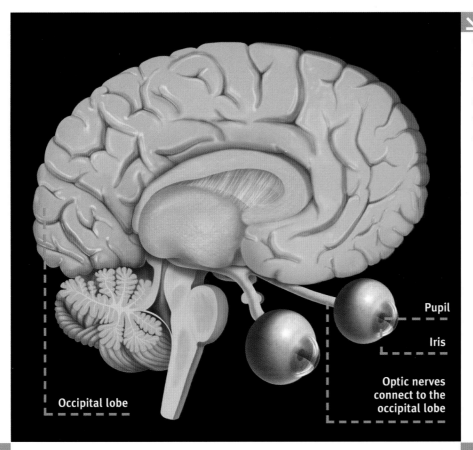

Occipital lobe

Pupil

Iris

Optic nerves connect to the occipital lobe

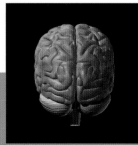

Your eyes are really an extension of your brain. When you look at something, it's your brain that's seeing it, not your eyeballs.

helps you determine distances and keeps you from bumping into things.

These control centers for the different functions of the body and mind are spread out across the entire cortex: some in front, some on the sides, some in back, and some on top. The speech section is far removed from the visual section. So how do the two communicate with each other so that people can talk about what they are seeing? For that matter, how does any one part of the brain send information to another?

THE WHITE MATTER (INNER BRAIN)

For the answer to that, we must go to the next layer of the brain, the mushy inner section. This part of the brain is called the white matter. Unlike the gray matter, which appears pink, the white matter really is white. That's because it is composed of axons, long wirelike strands that connect nerve cells. And like a lot of everyday wires—such as

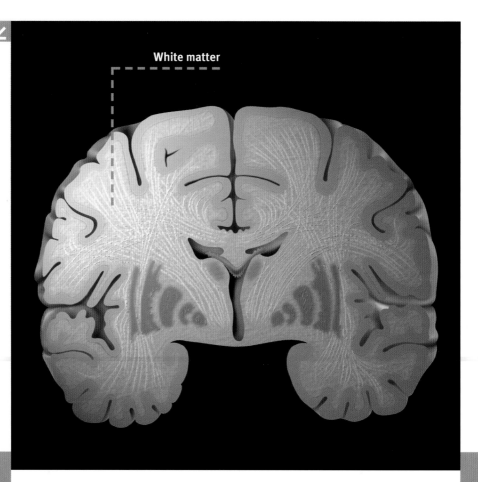

White matter

the wires in electrical cords or telephone cables—axons are wrapped in a protective coating or sheath. This axon coating is called myelin, which is made of shiny white fat. There is so much myelin—because there are so many axons—it makes this part of the brain look white.

The axons in the white matter link different parts of the cortex, like the speech area to the hearing area, and also link the other parts of the brain. The white matter works the same way a telephone switching system works. Some of the axons are direct connections, while others go through certain brain parts before spreading out again. No real thinking or activity happens here in the white matter; these are only the pathways for the communication that takes place in the brain. You can also think of the white matter as roads and highways that are connected all across your brain. If you picture a road map of the country, some of the roads might run from New York City to San Francisco, while others run only from New York City to nearby towns, or from San Francisco to

Los Angeles. Just like these roads leading out of cities, lots of the brain gets connected to a lot more of the brain via the intricate pathways that run through the white matter.

The white matter is critically important in helping us become smarter. As far as scientists can tell, the more thinking we do—especially when it comes to learning new skills, playing new games, or trying to figure out new puzzles—the more connections our white matter creates to link the different parts of the brain. It's like building more roads to make driving around easier. When the brain needs to use more memories or develop new skills, the white matter links more of it together to help the process. The more you think, the more connections your brain creates—which helps make you smarter. Some of these connections are so crisscrossed and complicated that they look like a game of cat's cradle.

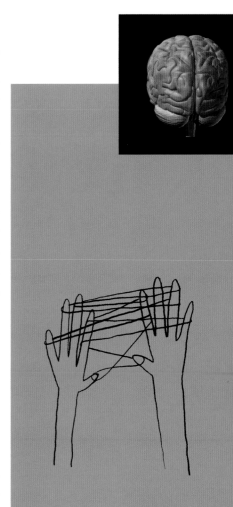

Connections occur more easily when you are young. That's why it's easier to learn a new language or skill when you're young. Someone who is forty years old has a pretty fixed set of connections, and making new ones isn't as easy for the brain as it used to be. So it's actually easier for a four-year-old than a forty-year-old to learn a new language.

While we're talking about connections in the white matter, it's a good time to look at how the two separate halves of the brain—the left and right hemispheres—are connected. Each hemisphere of the brain looks very much like the other one, from the gray matter all the way down into the white matter. There is very little difference because all the functions that the left brain needs to control the right side of your body have to also exist in the right brain, which controls the left side of your body.

But the two halves need to work together. Thinking functions, for instance, are spread out in different places across both hemispheres, while speech is contained mostly in the left brain. Plus, you have many parts of your body that need to work together as a single unit—you can't have the left leg trying to

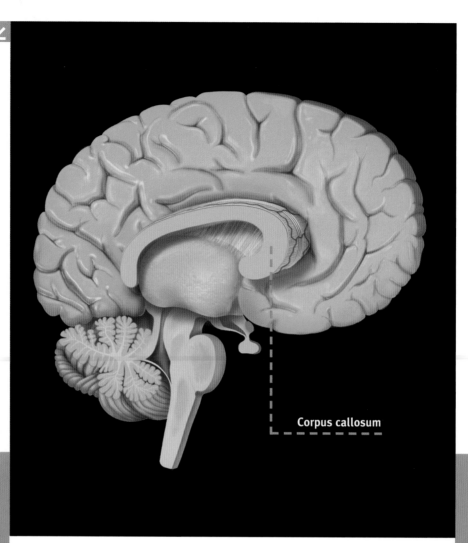

Corpus callosum

walk while the right leg waits around for something to do. There has to be communication between the two sides of the brain or else you might act like two different people.

Communications and connections between the left and right brains are made possible by a stretch of fibers called the corpus callosum. This part of the brain is located where the two hemispheres meet in the middle. It connects the parts of the left brain with the same parts in the right brain. It's like a thin sheet hung down the middle of a room that lets signals such as light and sound pass through. With the corpus callosum as the connection, the left hand knows what the right hand is doing, so to speak. All of the parts of the body can then work together, and all of the brain can think as one.

THE PRIMITIVE BRAIN

While the corpus callosum links two sides of the brain, the white matter links the thinking and reasoning part of the brain (the cortex) to the parts of the brain underneath the cortex. The parts underneath are called the primitive brain because they don't involve thinking. They are found in many creatures and have been around for millions of years. They were the first sections of the brain to evolve when creatures started "growing" brains. The primitive brain controls things like survival, instincts, and the basic functions of the body, such as hunger, heartbeat, and breathing.

THE LIMBIC SYSTEM—THE MAMMALIAN BRAIN

The first part of the primitive brain that we encounter—once we dig our way past the white matter—is called the limbic system. It is the center of memory and emotion, so it is often called the "emotional brain." It is also called the mammalian brain because it's the part of the brain that we share with many mammals, including our prehistoric ancestors. The limbic system is made up of several pieces—some of which reach into other parts of the brain—but the ones we're most interested in here are the hippocampus, the amygdala, and the olfactory system. These parts of the limbic system are tucked in between the two temporal lobes. Even though they are in the center section between the two lobes, these parts are still duplicated: Like the rest of the brain, there are two hippocampi, two amygdalae, and two olfactory systems, one for each side of the brain.

HIPPOCAMPUS—AND MEMORY

The hippocampus is small and curvy and shaped like a sea horse—although the name makes it sound like it should be shaped like a hippopotamus. But hippocampus actually means "sea horse" in Latin. The hippocampus is extremely important because it is the part of your brain that controls how your memories are stored and whether or not you are able to remember things.

Controller and Connections

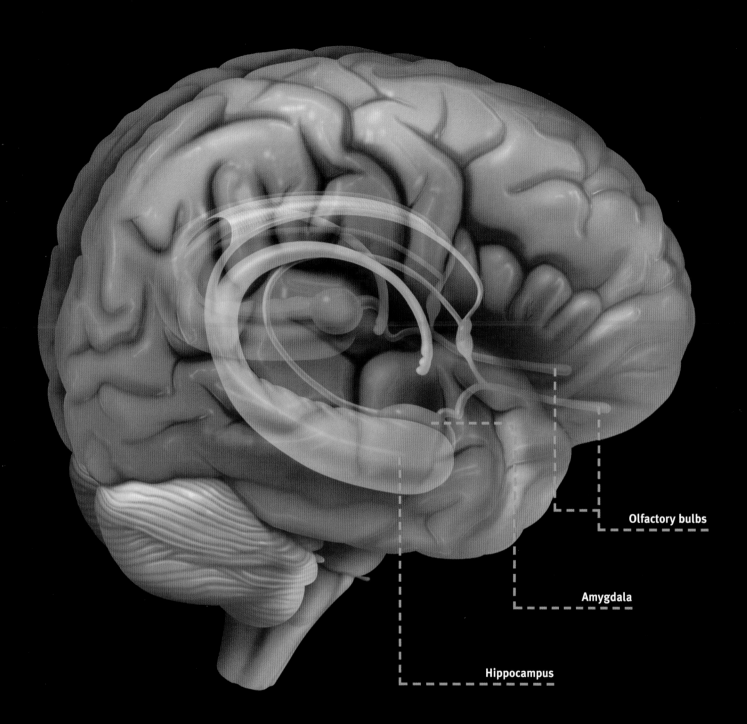

Olfactory bulbs

Amygdala

Hippocampus

↖ The limbic system is called the mammalian brain because it is similar to the type of brain found in many mammals. Our emotions are controlled here, and our memories are stored here.

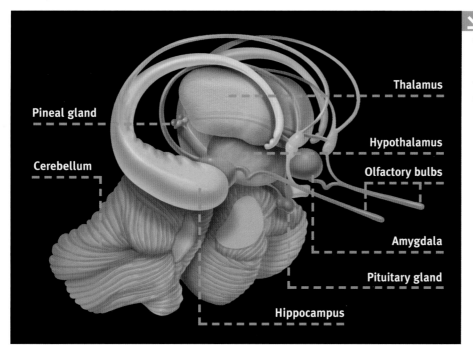

Pineal gland

Cerebellum

Thalamus

Hypothalamus

Olfactory bulbs

Amygdala

Pituitary gland

Hippocampus

The hippocampus is where your memories are sorted and stored. Can you remember that?

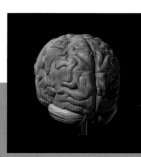

There are three types of memories. The first is called working, or short-term, memory. It helps you remember the name of a person you just met, or what you had for lunch a few minutes ago, or a phone number someone just told you to dial. It doesn't last long—only a few seconds or minutes—that's why it's called "short-term." Short-term memories are usually things that you'll forget five minutes after you've heard or seen them.

The second memory type is declarative, or long-term, memory—also called fact memory. This allows you to remember what your first-grade teacher's name was, or the name of your elementary school, or the name of your favorite toy when you were little. This is the memory you use when you want to remember facts and figures (even if they are useless) or when you take a test at the end of the school year. A short-term memory can actually become a long-term memory if it is used frequently, like the phone number of someone you call every day.

The third is procedural, or skills, memory. It is the memory responsible for recalling skills that you've learned over a long time. These kinds of memories are almost impossible to forget because your body and brain have worked so hard to create them. This is the

DÉJÀ VU

The hippocampus is responsible for routing memories to long- and short-term destinations. But what happens if the hippocampus doesn't get it right? There is an interesting theory about memories that involves a mix-up in the hippocampus. If you've ever gone to a new place and felt like you've been there before, it's called *déjà vu*. This is a French term meaning "already seen," and it means that you feel like you've been somewhere or done something when you really haven't. Some scientists think that this might happen when the hippocampus sends a new experience directly into long-term memory instead of treating it as a short-term memory. So when you experience déjà vu, your brain is treating the event as an old memory even though it just happened, simply because your hippocampus misfiled it.

memory that helps you remember how to play a musical instrument or throw a football or button the buttons on your shirt.

It's important to understand the difference between these types of memories because the hippocampus decides which ones will get sorted where. For instance, what you had for breakfast isn't that important to your brain, so the hippocampus sends it to short-term memory. It's soon forgotten, and it's unlikely you will ever remember what you had for breakfast a week ago (unless it was something truly unusual).

On the other hand, if you burn your finger on a hot toaster, your hippocampus will decide that you'd better remember that—you'll need to avoid touching hot toasters in the future—and will send the information to long-term memory, which is stored in the cortex.

Memories that are based on physical repetition or that are part of learning a skill—like playing a guitar or tying your shoelaces or riding a bike—appear to be stored in the cerebellum. We'll get to the cerebellum in a moment; it's an area that is even deeper in the brain.

Memory storage happens without you knowing it. Here's a test to show how quickly you can forget things (and don't look). What color are the socks you put on today? What about yesterday? How many sips did you take from your last glass of milk? How many times did you raise your hand in class yesterday? Odds are that you can't remember any of these things right off the bat—if at all.

How about facts from long ago? What was your kindergarten teacher's name? What was the name of the last restaurant you went to? You can remember these things because they are either important facts or special events. And even though they happened longer ago than when you put on your socks, your brain still keeps memories of them around.

The hippocampus sorts memories every second of the day. And it does a good job. The stuff you need to remember—people's names, math facts, your home telephone number—all get stored in the right place, while things that would clog up your brain, like remembering the color of the clothes you wore three days ago, get "erased" quickly.

AMYGDALA—THE EMOTIONAL CENTER

Tucked at the end of the hippocampus is a knobby little bit of tissue called the amygdala. This little nub is where your emotional center is. When you're feeling glad, sad, mad, or bad, those emotions are generated in the amygdala. It is also called the fear center. One of your strongest emotions—whether you know it or not—is fear. Fear is necessary for survival, although more for animals than people. But humans have to learn to be careful of things every day, whether it's looking out for traffic when you're crossing a street or being extra careful when climbing a tree.

The amygdala interprets nonverbal information from your senses. This means images, sounds, and smells, but not words. The amygdala compares incoming information with your past experiences, and then decides what your body should do about a serious or scary situation. The amygdala determines whether you face up to something or decide that it's smarter and safer to run away. This is called the "fight or flight" response. This happens before your thinking brain—the cortex—can get involved. It's why you jump when somebody suddenly scares you, or why you flinch when something like a baseball, a bee, or a fist flies near your head. The amygdala tells your body to move before your cortex gets the information. If you had to stand and think about what to do in these situations, you might not make a decision fast enough. The amygdala acts like your safety autopilot and takes over when you're in danger.

For example, if you happen to see an angry rhinoceros charging toward you, the amygdala would compare this event to memories and knowledge you have ("a charging rhinoceros is a dangerous thing, and it could crush me like a bug"), and then send information to other parts of the brain about how to react ("increase heartbeat, send energy to muscles, run away as fast as you can!").

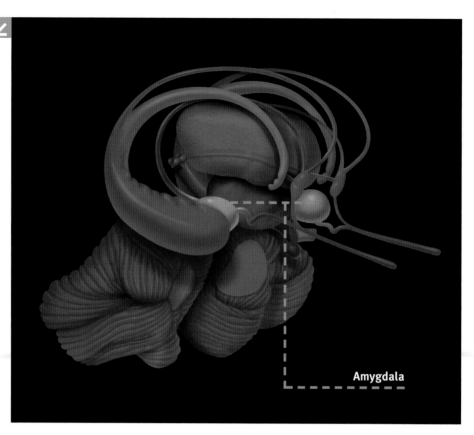

The amygdala is the part of the brain that can save your life in dangerous situations.

Amygdala

The amygdala is also responsible for how you handle other emotions, including excitement, guilt, pleasure, sorrow, anger, and jealousy. By working with different long-term memories, it helps ensure that you respond appropriately to various situations you find yourself in. If the amygdala wasn't working, you might see that charging rhinoceros and decide to go give it a big hug. Or you might run away screaming when someone smiles at you.

These two parts of the limbic system, the hippocampus and the amygdala, work together to help you understand and deal with your feelings and other people's feelings. As humans, we rely a great deal on our emotions—whether we're angry or sad, scared or happy—and this part of the brain keeps it all in order. Because it deals with nonverbal information, the amygdala must interpret social situations, including reading the emotions on another person's face or understanding how another person is behaving. Damage to the amygdala prevents a person from understanding the look on someone else's face. The person can't tell that a smile means happiness or that a frown means anger.

Scientists believe our emotions can be broken down into six basic types: happiness, sadness, anger, surprise, disgust, and fear. Interestingly, we show each of these emotions by one of six specific looks on our faces. This is why the amygdala can handle the interpretation of our nonverbal emotions. And making these faces is not something we learn; it's part of all of us. Even people who have never been able to see make these faces when they experience certain emotions.

Sometimes, though, emotions can overwhelm us to the point where we are too scared to move or too excited to pay attention. Then we actually have to force ourselves—using the reasoning centers in our cortex—to overcome these emotions. It's up to the thinking brain to overrule the limbic system and allow us to take control of our behavior and movements.

OLFACTORY SYSTEM

The next part of the limbic region that we'll examine is involved with smell. It is called the olfactory system. It may seem a little strange to have the sense of smell buried down here in the primitive brain, but scientists think this is because smell is one of the oldest senses, one that many creatures rely on more than other senses. Smell is directly connected to your temporal lobe through a pathway that begins with the olfactory bulbs. Because it has a direct link to your thinking brain, smell is considered "hardwired" into your brain.

People don't rely on their sense of smell as much as animals do. Creatures like sharks and dogs use their sense of smell much more than they use their eyes. But smell is something that was vital to our ancestors in the past. This is why it still has such a strong link to our brains. Today, our olfactory system helps us identify thousands of different odors. These range from foods and flavors to the scent of other people. Every person—except twins— has a different scent, and babies can even recognize the scent of

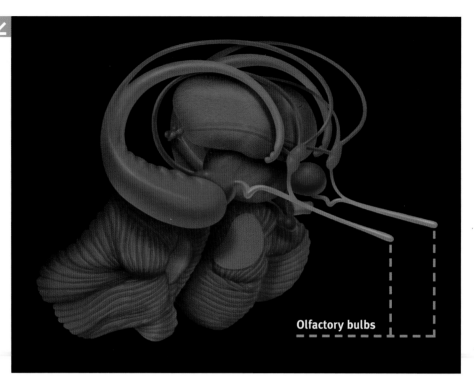

Smells take an express route into the thinking brain, courtesy of the olfactory tract.

Olfactory bulbs

their own mothers. The olfactory system also alerts us to odors that should be avoided, such as foul water, rancid meat, and rotten vegetables.

THALAMUS AND HYPOTHALAMUS

Let's keep going deeper into the brain. The next section of the brain is composed of tiny separate structures that work to keep our bodies comfortable and on schedule—controlling functions such as temperature, growth, sleepiness, and hunger. The first two of these structures are the thalamus and hypothalamus, which are connected to both the cerebellum and the brain stem. These two bits of brain get you through your day—literally.

Most of the senses are actually connected to the thalamus, a little switchboard that handles how sensory data reaches the brain (we'll get to that in a moment). The thalamus is composed of two parts that look like tiny footballs joined by a small bridge, making it look like a bloated letter *H*. It is the gateway to your cortex. Most of the sensory information (except smell) that your body receives passes through it. The thalamus sends signals from the body to

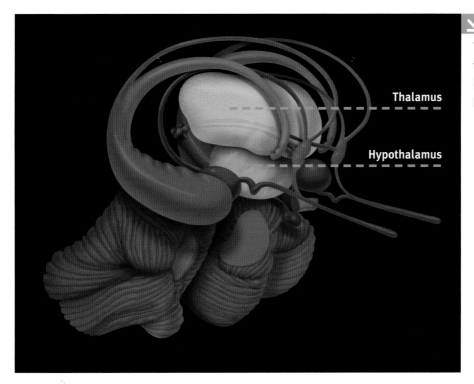

Thalamus

Hypothalamus

The thalamus directs traffic in your brain. The hypothalamus keeps your body on schedule.

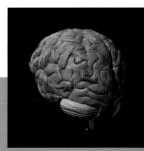

the brain and at the same time sends signals from the brain to the body. Just like a traffic cop controls the movement of traffic, creating a rhythm of stops and starts, the thalamus keeps the body moving smoothly.

Underneath this traffic cop is the hypothalamus. The hypothalamus is your "internal clock" and controls your body's schedule. It determines when you need to sleep, when you get hungry and need to eat, and when you are thirsty. If your body is running low on fluids, the hypothalamus sends out messages that tell you you're thirsty. It sends hunger messages, too. You don't get hungry because your stomach is empty; you get hungry because your brain needs nutrients. Your hypothalamus sends you the message that you need to eat something to get those nutrients.

The hypothalamus also acts as a thermostat and maintains control of your body's internal temperature. If you're too hot, it expands the capillaries in your skin. This allows your blood to be cooled faster, which then cools the rest of your body as the blood flows back to your heart.

Controller and Connections

Interestingly, our internal body clocks may not really be best suited to a twenty-four-hour day. Our bodies have adapted to this cycle because that's a time schedule based on the sun rising and setting. But people who have spent time without any exposure to sunlight, in places such as the Arctic where there is no sunshine in the winter, or in controlled laboratories where there is no light change between day and night, find that their body clocks don't match up to twenty-four hours. Instead, their days stretch up to thirty hours or more for a normal cycle. This means the amount of time between when they wake up is thirty hours. Without sunlight as a guide, it appears that we might be naturally suited to longer days.

Keeping you awake, alert, and in tune with your day is what the hypothalamus does best. Contrary to what you might think, the twenty-four-hour clock we live by is not set by our watches and alarm clocks. It is a natural body cycle that coincides with the length of a day, from the time the sun rises, past when it gets dark, to when it comes up again. At various points during the day, the hypothalamus kicks certain organs into gear and slows down others.

For example, when you're about to wake up, it jump-starts your heartbeat, your breathing, and your kidneys. Soon after you wake up, your hypothalamus sends your body a message that it needs fuel in the form of protein to get all its parts moving. This translates to you as "breakfast." Within about an hour after waking up, your entire body is ready to work at full speed. As you get about four hours into your day, it signals your body's need for food (which is timed nicely for lunch), and then slows down the body again to help digest that food. This is why people sometimes take naps after lunch even if they weren't sleepy before. At night, it slows your heartbeat and breathing rate, and when you're asleep, everything is set to the slowest speed of the day.

Responses to emotions also come from this part of the limbic system. If someone is yelling at you, the sounds are transferred from the thalamus to the cortex, which figures out what is being said. Then a message goes to the hypothalamus, which decides how your body is going to react. Maybe the yelling is making you angry, so the hypothalamus instructs your blood pressure to rise. Maybe it makes you nervous, so the hypothalamus tells your body to sweat and your heart to beat faster. If your cortex—your thinking brain—decides that the person who is yelling is just ridiculous, the hypothalamus may instruct your body to laugh out loud.

PITUITARY AND PINEAL GLANDS

Hanging out in front of the thalamus is a little pea-sized gland called the pituitary. Even though it is tiny, the pituitary is one of the most important glands in your body (other important glands are your sweat glands, salivary glands, and adrenal glands). The pituitary

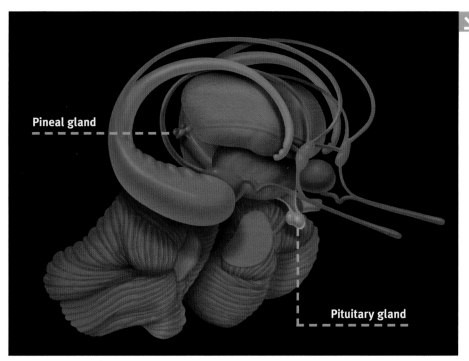

Pineal gland

Pituitary gland

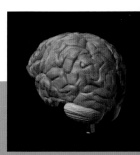

The pituitary gland is one of the tiniest components of the brain, but it decides how big you will be.

releases hormones into your body that determine how tall or short you will be, and how fast or slow you will grow. It also has some say about when you start puberty, affects how high or how deep your voice will be, and when hair will start growing on various parts of your body. The pituitary works with the hypothalamus to keep your body on a regular cycle of growth throughout your life.

A little farther back in the brain, tucked into a ventricle, is another gland called the pineal. It releases the hormone melatonin, which is important for switching your sleep cycles on and off. We don't know a lot about the pineal gland, but apparently it senses the time of day based on how much light your brain is receiving through your eyes. When it starts getting dark at night the pineal gland goes into action. Because it responds to light and dark signals, it is sometimes called your "third eye."

Scientists are still investigating how the parts of the primitive brain work together. We aren't sure how they share information or coordinate their functions. We know a lot about the cortex because it is on the outside of the brain and can be touched and observed during surgery. But the limbic system and the parts around it are so deep

inside the brain and so tightly packed together that doctors can't get to those parts in living patients. Experimenting or performing surgery in this area could severely interrupt the body's basic functions and possibly cause permanent damage and even death.

◥ THE CEREBELLUM

At the base of the brain, just under the back of the cerebrum, is the cerebellum. (It's easy to confuse these two brain parts because of their names. It helps to remember that cerebellum means "little cerebrum.") Like the cerebrum, the cerebellum is covered by the cortex and divided into a left side and a right side. The cerebellum is about the size of a golf ball and is shaped like a clump of cauliflower, making it the biggest part of the brain after the individual lobes. If you put your hand at the back of your head right on the bony base of your skull, your cerebellum is located right above that.

The cerebellum is responsible for coordinating all your movements and motions. When you reach out to pick up a glass of water, when you ride a bike, when you walk up the stairs, when you rub your eyes, when you simply stand still—and try to keep your balance—your cerebellum is handling it all.

The cerebellum not only handles the basic movements of your body, but it monitors and coordinates all the movements you make. It makes sure that all parts of your body work together smoothly, instead of every part of you going its own way. That's why your fingers can turn the page of this book when your hand reaches out, while your elbow balances your forearm and your wrist, and your shoulder supports your whole arm.

The cerebellum has more nerve cells than any other part of the brain. These cells allow the cerebellum to act like your body's autopilot, doing things that, if you thought about them, you probably couldn't do. Try to think about how you ride a bike. It's hard to describe in detail. It's much easier to get on a bike and just ride. This is because your cerebellum knows how to coordinate

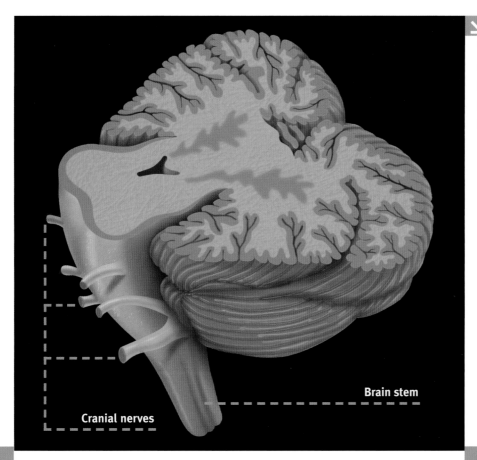

This is the cerebellum with the top lopped off. It has wrinkles and a cortex just like the cerebrum.

Cranial nerves

Brain stem

your body's balance along with the pumping of your legs, the tilt of your head, the way you watch the road in front of you, and the way you use your shoulders, arms, and hands to steer the handlebars. It can coordinate these movements better than your thinking brain can describe them. When you tell somebody, "It's easier if I just show you," that's the cerebellum in action.

The cerebellum and the cerebrum keep in close contact, working together like a pilot and copilot sitting side-by-side in an airplane. When you decide you need to do something, the thought starts in your cerebral cortex. The cortex sends messages to your body via the brain stem. The cerebellum monitors these messages to make sure that your body obeys your brain's commands. It keeps all your muscles and nerves working in time with one another, and makes tiny adjustments that you don't even think about. It even maintains control over barely noticeable muscle movements, such as how your lips and tongue are moving to form the words your brain wants to say. If you're slurring

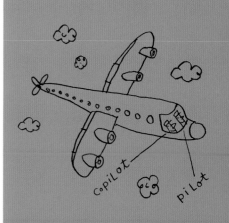

Controller and Connections

your words or having trouble pronouncing them, the cerebellum makes corrections to how the muscles in your lips and tongue move to produce clear speech.

The cerebellum has its own regulator that checks on how it's doing. Located in front of the cerebellum, close to the center of your brain, are the basal ganglia. This is a group of nerves that acts as the brake to the cerebellum's motor. The basal ganglia keep your movements from going out of control. They keep the orders that the cerebellum sends to the body in line with what the cortex wants. If you're running a race or jumping over hurdles, for example, you need to keep your feet a certain distance from each other. If your feet move too far ahead of each other, you will trip and fall. The basal ganglia help you keep your balance by providing balance to the cerebellum.

THE BRAIN STEM—THE REPTILIAN BRAIN

Sticking down from the cerebrum, right in front of the cerebellum, is the brain stem. It connects the brain to the spinal cord. All the messages that go back and forth between the brain and the body have to pass along the brain stem. It also handles the body's most basic functions. In fact, you could stay alive without every other part of your brain (although you wouldn't want to), but you couldn't live without your brain stem.

In primitive animals, the brain stem is just about all the brain there is. All the other parts we've talked about in the human brain just don't exist for these creatures. This is why your brain stem is sometimes referred to as the "reptilian brain," because it's the main part of the brain in creatures such as lizards, turtles, and fish.

The brain stem keeps you alive without you thinking about it. Just imagine if you had to think about every single thing your body does: breathe in, breathe out, heartbeat, heartbeat, breathe in, breathe out, blink, heartbeat, heartbeat, blink, breathe in. . . . You couldn't keep track of it all. So the responsibility for the basic functions of your body falls to the brain stem. It works with the

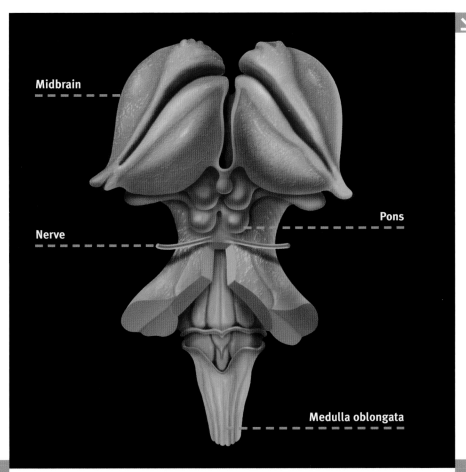

Midbrain

Nerve

Pons

Medulla oblongata

limbic system to keep your heartbeat, blood pressure, body temperature, and other functions at normal levels.

The brain stem is also like a pole on which parts of the brain are hung. In addition to all of the pieces attached to it, most of the big nerves in your head, called the cranial nerves, run through the brain stem. These nerves are responsible for all of the movements in your head, from the movement of your eyes to the way you swallow your food.

The brain stem is divided into three parts. The first is the midbrain. It is at the top of the brain stem and is shaped a little like a hook. It contains nerves that send information from the eyes and ears to the thalamus. It also controls head and eye movement, two of the most important movements in your entire body. Because of this, the midbrain has more motor nerves than any other section of your central nervous system.

BOMBARDING THE RETICULAR FORMATION

Your eyes see by using tiny receptors called rods and cones. There are more than five million cones and more than 120 million rods sending signals to your brain. These signals tell your brain about everything you see, from colors and shadows to movement and depth.

There are ten thousand taste buds in your mouth, mostly on your tongue. Each one has fifty to one hundred and fifty receptors. That means that your mouth can send more than a million signals to your brain while you're eating something.

Your ears capture sound waves and send them to your brain via a complex system of small hairs and liquid. Neurons turn these waves into signals and your brain identifies the signals as sounds.

Your hand has 17,000 receptors that give you your sense of touch. The skin that covers your body has receptors along every inch of it, although not every part is as sensitive as your hand.

Add all this up, and it means that your brain is receiving several hundred million bits of information every second—even at this very moment. The reticular formation sorts out what's important and what's not.

One of the coolest things about the midbrain is that it shuts out most of the world when you are asleep, like locking a door to the rest of the body. During sleep, the midbrain allows almost no external stimuli to get into your brain, unless that stimulus is loud (like thunder), exceptionally bright (like an overhead light), or touching you (like someone grabbing your arm).

Right below your midbrain is a bulging mass, like a swollen throat, called the pons. The pons connects the cerebral cortex above the brain stem to the medulla oblongata below it. Scientists have found that the pons is what sends you into rapid eye movement, or REM, sleep, the phase of sleep when you dream.

Right below the swollen pons is the medulla oblongata. This long stretch of cord provides a pathway for motor signals between the nerves in the spinal cord and the brain. It is the main center of breathing and heart control, but it is also the place where activities you can't always control are taken care of—like swallowing, coughing, gagging, and even vomiting.

Now, here's one of the most curious facts about the brain stem: It probably keeps your brain from overloading thanks to groups of nerve cells, called the reticular formation, which run up and down the brain stem. Because the reticular formation is spread out over the brain stem and isn't just in a single section, it is rarely talked about. But when all its nerves work together, the reticular formation keeps you focused on what you're doing.

The reticular formation is like a filter for the thalamus. This means that it limits the information that gets admitted into your brain. Its job is to take the millions of sensory inputs you get every second from all over your body—eyes, ears, nose, mouth, fingertips, skin—and let in only the important stuff. What's important and what's not important is up to the reticular formation.

The reticular formation allows musicians onstage to focus on their singing or playing even when thousands of fans are screaming and waving at them. It allows athletes who have been slightly injured during a game to keep playing. It allows you to listen only to the words your friends are saying in a crowded cafeteria—even when hundreds of other kids are talking and making a lot of noise. If you had to listen to every other conversation, along with the clanking of plates and forks and glasses, and then think about what it all meant, it would make you feel like your head was going to explode.

Now think about this: When you're wearing a headband, a watch, socks, or a belt, your body probably can't "feel" that you're wearing them. You can feel them when you put them on because while you were focusing on them, your skin receptors sent messages to your brain. But after a few moments, your reticular formation stopped sending this information along. It's not important for your brain to know that your belt and socks are on every second (until something happens to them—like if they fall off!).

The midbrain, the pons, and the medulla oblongata make up the brain stem, which is an incredibly busy place. Because so much information about our world and what we're doing goes through the brain stem, scientists call it a "high traffic area." It is here that we've finally reached the end of the brain because the brain stem serves as both the entrance and the exit tunnel into and out of the brain.

THE SPINAL CORD

On its way out of the brain, the brain stem connects the brain with the spinal cord. The spinal cord, in turn, connects the entire brain with the rest of the body. An interesting thing about this connection point between brain and spinal cord is the way the nerves are separated. All the nerves from the left side of the body cross over to the right brain, and all the nerves from the right side of the body cross over to the left brain. This crossover is why the left brain controls the right side of the body and vice versa.

The spinal cord is a big part of the central nervous system. It is a group of nerve bundles that goes down the center of the spine to

Even though I'm wearing a hat and my cowboy outfit, I don't feel them, or think about them when I'm playing the Banjo.

the middle of your back. At the end of the spinal cord, long strands of nerve roots, called the *cauda equina* (which means "horse's tail" because of the way it looks), reach down through your spine. From there, nerve fibers connect to the rest of your body—to every finger, toe, muscle, and patch of skin. The spinal cord holds the nerve fibers in one place so there is one main line of communication between your brain and your body.

The spinal cord, working with a small part of the brain stem, is also responsible for your autonomic nervous system, or the ANS. It keeps information going to the "automatic" organs in your body, like your heart, lungs, bladder, and even the pupils in your eyes—organs that have to work continuously no matter how you're feeling or what you're thinking. In some cases, the normal day-to-day signals from these organs don't even have to make it all the way into the brain—the ANS has them on autopilot.

↘ BLOOD IN YOUR BRAIN

Everything we've talked about so far shows how nerve information comes into and goes out of your brain and how that information is handled. But something else has to come in and out of your brain in order for it to work: blood. Next to the hole where the spinal cord enters your skull, there are little holes where the blood supply comes into the brain. Two sets of arteries, the internal carotid arteries and the vertebral arteries, snake up into your skull. They continuously pump blood containing nutrients and fuel, such as glucose and oxygen, into your brain.

The brain needs a lot of blood, more than any other part of your body. Almost twenty percent of all the fresh blood in your body goes straight to your brain, pumped by your heart through the arteries. Your brain is always first in line to get the oxygen carried by blood because every part of your body depends on the brain working properly. Without oxygen, a brain quickly loses power. And without your brain telling your body how to work, the body shuts down, like a car that's out of gas.

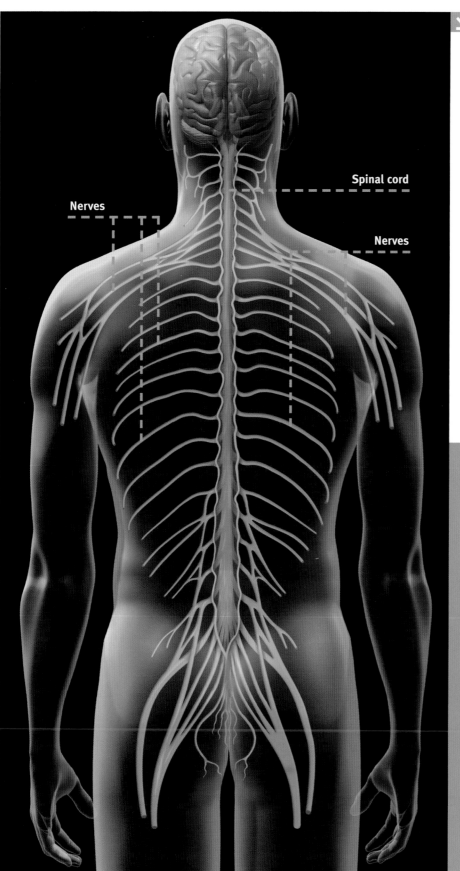

Spinal cord

Nerves

Nerves

The spinal cord is the central corridor that connects the nerves in your body to your brain. Nerves (shown in yellow) branch out from the spinal cord, which is protected by bones called vertebrae.

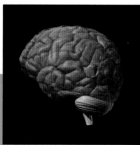

Controller and Connections

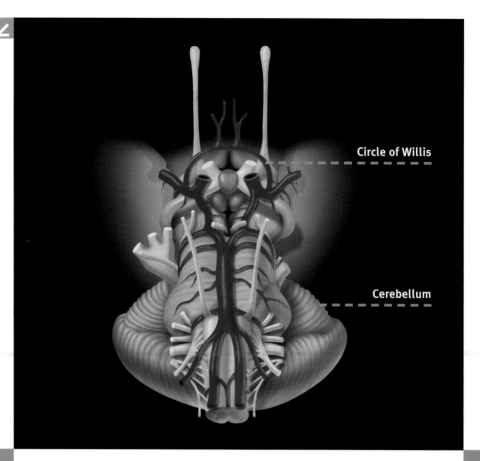

Circle of Willis

Cerebellum

To make sure that blood always gets to the brain—even if some of the arteries become clogged or blocked or damaged—there is a unique ring of arterial connections in the brain. This ring is called the circle of Willis, after Thomas Willis, the man who wrote the first textbook on the brain. The circle provides several different pathways of blood into the brain, like different ramps leading to the same highway, so that if one artery is damaged, there are still plenty of other pathways into the brain.

Now you've traveled through all the major parts of your brain. You've gotten the big picture, and you've broken it down into its basic components, from gray matter and white matter to the limbic system, cerebellum, and brain stem. Now it's time to see these things in action. And in order to do that, we have to start with the microscopic cell that holds the key to everything your brain does: the neuron.

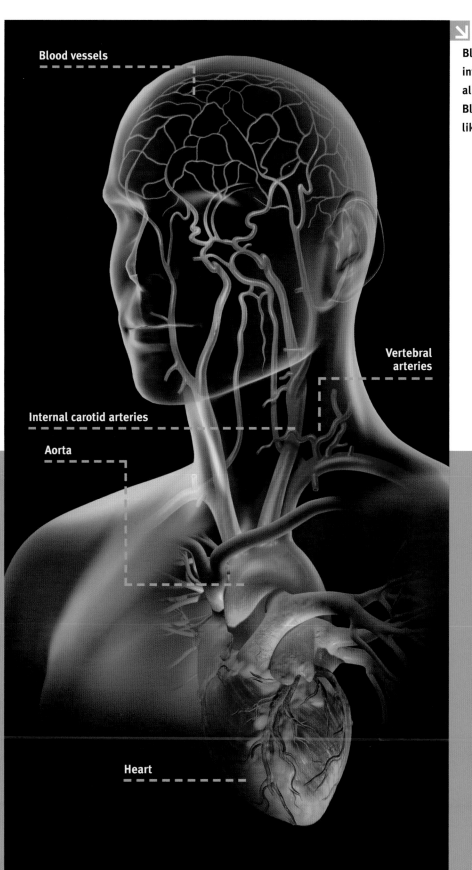

Blood vessels

Vertebral arteries

Internal carotid arteries

Aorta

Heart

Blood vessels snake up into your head and wrap all around your brain. Blood is the brain's fuel, like gas for a car.

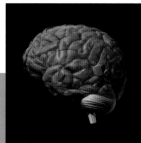

YOUR BRAIN IN ACTION

Let's see what happens in your brain when you do something almost everyone likes to do: watch a movie.

■ Start by imagining that you're in a movie theater. You've come to see the biggest movie of the year and you're excited. Everybody has been talking about this movie, and you're finally getting to see it.

■ You sit down in your seat. You've got a big bucket of popcorn and an extra-large soda, and the lights have dimmed. The film flickers to life. The show is starting. Here's what your brain makes of the situation:

■ Images of actors appear on the screen. Light that is moving at 186,000 miles per second comes from the screen and hits your eyes. The cones and rods in your eyeballs send millions of signals along the optic nerve to your thalamus. Your eyes are moving back and forth, up and down, in little movements so that you take in everything on the screen. Your brain is piecing it all together. Think about this the next time you watch a movie: Because of the size of the screen, you can't see the whole picture at once, so your eyes dart around the screen. The muscles that move your eyeballs are being controlled by commands from your cerebellum.

■ At the same time, you're listening to the first words the actors say. The speakers in the theater make the sound fairly loud, about 70 decibels (60 decibels is normal conversation). The words come from the speakers on the wall and bounce into your head off the flappy part of your outer ear. Millions of cilia in your ear canal jiggle slightly and sound waves ripple through your inner ear, creating vibrations that your neurons turn into impulses. These impulses hit your thalamus at almost exactly the same time as the images from your optic nerve.

■ The messages from your eyes and ears get sent through the thalamus and into the cortex. The visual messages go to the optical cortex in the back of your brain, while the sound messages go to the sides of your brain, over toward Broca's and Wernicke's areas. From there, messages in your brain start zipping back and forth through the white matter and across the corpus callosum to combine the words with what you're seeing. This is all happening at approximately 268 miles an hour, or about four times as fast as a car drives on the highway.

■ Your brain reaches into memory areas where your long-term memories are stored and makes sense of the words, so that what you see and hear make sense at the same time. In addition, the hippocampus is tracking the action on the screen, and making decisions about what's worth keeping in long-term memory. If it's a good joke, or an action scene, it might store this part of the movie in your declarative memory. But much of the dialogue and detail will go to the short-term memory area and will be gone in a few minutes. There's no way you'll be able to remember the movie word-for-word after it's over.

■ Meanwhile, the smell of the popcorn enters your nostrils. Actually, the smell is made up of molecules of butter. These race up your nose and into your olfactory tract. The olfactory tract sends nerve impulses straight into the brain's temporal lobe, bypassing the various traffic cops in the midbrain.

■ The smell stimulates both the cortex and parts of your limbic system. They send a message to your salivary glands, which start your mouth watering. This triggers desire for the popcorn in the cortex, which thinks, "I'd really like to eat some popcorn."

■ The motor strip of the cortex sends a message to the cerebellum, which sends a message down to your arm and hand to reach into the popcorn bucket. But you're looking at the screen, not the popcorn. So the cerebellum and basal ganglia make sure that your hand finds its way into the popcorn bucket. Your fingers move around, and their nerve endings are informing your brain, especially the somatosensory strip, that they've found the popcorn. Another command goes down to the hand to grab some, but not too hard, or you'll crumble the popcorn into bits—and not too many, or they'll fall in your lap.

■ Your cerebellum then guides your hand to your mouth. Messages have been sent to your mouth to get ready, so saliva is flowing. As your fingers drop the popcorn into your mouth, your tongue, lips, teeth, jaw muscles, and throat all begin to move, working together to get that popcorn into your stomach.

■ Suddenly, something scary happens on the screen. You weren't expecting it, and neither was your brain. The surprise—or the shock— goes straight to your amygdala, which responds by putting your entire body on alert. Your body jerks, your eyes bug out,

and some of the popcorn drops from your hand. This is something you can't control. It's built into your body, probably from tens of thousands of years of evolution. If this wasn't a movie, the shock would make you ready to stand and fight—or turn and run. The hypothalamus is sending messages down to your heart, making it beat faster, pumping more blood to your muscles. It tells your lungs to speed up as well because the heart needs to send more fresh blood to your body and brain, and it takes oxygen to make blood fresh.

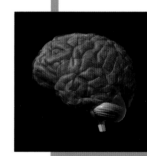

■ The reason the movie is having such an impact on you is that your reticular formation has focused you completely on the movie. You don't see the light shining on the faces of people sitting next to you, you don't hear the hum of the theater's air-conditioning, and you barely notice anything else except the screen (unless someone talks really loud or a cell phone rings). Your focus is so intense that minor distractions don't even affect you.

As you can see, the brain is extremely busy even when you're doing something as simple and relaxing as watching a movie. Think of how busy it must be when you're taking a test or playing a game or learning a new skill.

Neurons: one Hundred Trillion connections

Your body is made up of cells. You already knew that. But the cells in your brain are not like the other cells in your body. ↗

5 neurons: one hundred trillion connections

CHAPTER
FIVE

To start with, brain cells have a specific name. They are called neurons. There are one hundred billion of these neurons in your brain. That's 100,000,000,000—a 1 with eleven zeroes behind it.

There are different types of neurons in each part of your brain, but they are all similar. Like most of your body's cells, each one is composed of a cell body with a nucleus. Surrounding the cell body are dendrites, which look like lots of spider legs. And snaking out of the cell body is an axon, which looks like a long tail.

What makes neurons unusual is the way they connect and communicate with one another. Unlike other cells, neurons don't touch one another—they are separated by open spaces called synapses. Neurons communicate with one another across the synapses by creating chemical explosions that blast from one cell to the next. It's sort of like sending messages with fireworks.

Almost two hundred years ago, scientists guessed that all living things were made up of tiny building blocks called cells. In the mid-1800s, microscopes became powerful enough to allow scientists to see individual cells.

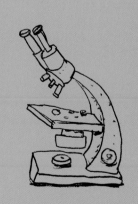

But the new microscopes didn't show individual brain cells. Some strange cell shapes could be seen, but they were so cluttered and

The Golgi stain turns only about one in ten neurons black. That makes individual neurons stand out like individual trees in a forest.

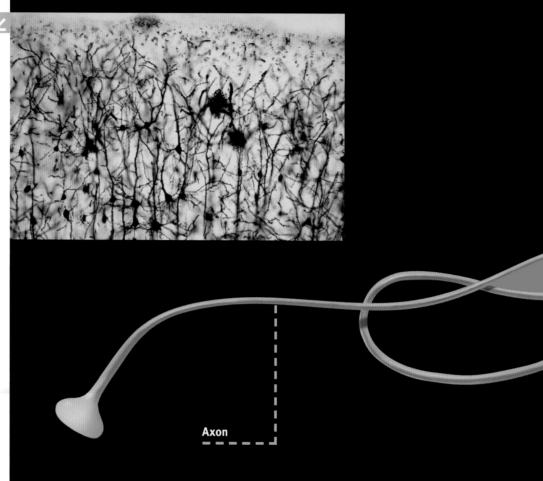

Axon

clumped together that scientists couldn't figure out what they were looking at. It was like looking through the thick branches of a huge tree. Quite simply, what they were seeing was too much of a mess to figure out. It took scientists a long time to figure out what the brain was made of—and to see what brain cells looked like. It wasn't until a man named Camillo Golgi accidentally dropped an owl brain into a strange mixture that scientists were finally able to see neurons.

The idea that the body was made of cells was only about forty years old when Golgi began his experiments. Although people realized that cells were the building blocks of tissue and skin, nobody thought that the brain was made of cells. And if it was, no one believed the brain would have specialized cells that were different from cells in other parts of the body.

Golgi did research on owl and cat brains, trying to find out if there was something that made their brain cells different from the rest of their cells. One day sometime in the 1870s—Golgi

Neurons

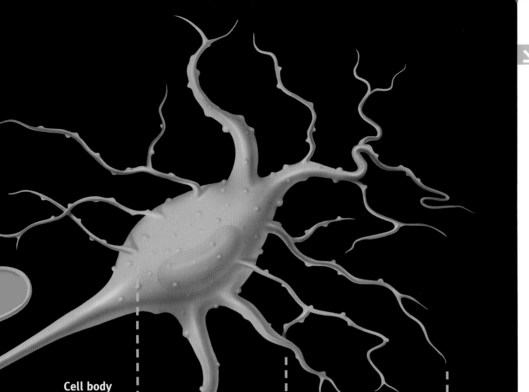

Cell body

Dendrites

never gave the exact date—he accidentally knocked part of an owl's brain into a solution of silver nitrate, a chemical solution used to prepare slides that would be looked at under a microscope. When he pulled the owl brain out of the solution and looked at it under a microscope, he was amazed. The silver nitrate had stained some, but not all, of the brain cells black. Golgi saw cells that were unlike any that had ever been seen before. They were neurons, the brain's specialized spiderlike cells, which resembled bare trees in a winter forest. Perhaps the strangest thing was their relationship to one another. Most cells in the body are clumped close to one another, like rooms in a hotel or in an apartment building. Their cell walls—the outside of the cell—touch the neighboring cells. But neurons don't touch their neighbors, at least not directly. Instead, they have long slinky strands that appear to connect one to the other. The strands branch out in many directions, sometimes skipping their neighbor and going on to touch as many as a thousand other cells (or almost touching—remember, neurons never physically

Neurons

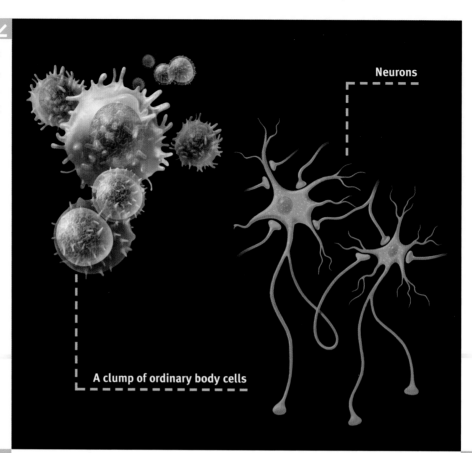

Most of your body's cells are clumped together, like the cells on the left. Neurons, on the right, get close but don't touch.

Neurons

A clump of ordinary body cells

touch one another). Some of these strands reach all the way across the entire brain.

These wiry strands make neurons unique. Over time, they were identified as the passageways that brought information into and out of the neuron's own little "brain," the nucleus. The strands are called neurites, and they come in two main types: axons and dendrites.

THE ELECTRICAL STORM

It was tough enough trying to see neurons under a microscope, so you can imagine how hard it was to then figure out how they function and work. Scientists wondered how such strange little specks could create thoughts, words, images, memories, dreams, and movement.

In 1891, a man named Heinrich Waldeyer came up with the idea that these cells sent messages to one another using their unique

Neurons

shape. He also made up the word "neuron" (which is derived from the Greek word for nerve) to describe the individual cells.

Waldeyer's theory was hard to prove. Brain researchers—called neuroscientists—couldn't watch a living brain under a microscope to figure out what it was doing. One thing neuroscientists did know, however, was that the brain seemed to be alive with electricity, as if there were little electrical storms occurring in every part of it. Neuroscientists wondered why.

As microscopes became more powerful, neuroscientists discovered that a gap exists between the end of an axon and the dendrites to which it is linked. They named this the synaptic gap, or the synapse. They deduced that the neurons must be communicating across that gap with electrical charges, like sparks jumping from one wire to the next. After all, spark plugs in machines work this way, sending a spark from a battery to a motor, so maybe that was the way it was with the brain. (Big secret: We still know a lot more about every machine ever invented than we do about our own brains.)

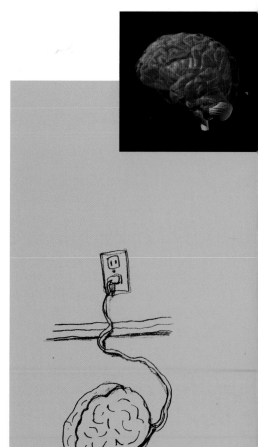

The first inkling that there was more to the brain's activity than just electricity came in 1921. That year, an Austrian researcher named Otto Loewi was working on frog nerves. He found that a frog's heart is controlled by two different nerves, one that slows it down and one that speeds it up. The problem was that each nerve used the same amount of electricity to perform its operation: It took as much electricity to start up as it did to slow down. That didn't make sense because slowing down would seem to take less energy, like slowing down a bike. Loewi believed that electricity was helping the nerves do their job, but that something else had to be controlling the speeding up or slowing down.

One night, Loewi had a dream about how chemicals might be used to speed up and slow down a frog's heart. Waking up in the middle of the night, he wrote down the details of his dream. He was shocked, though, when he woke up the next morning and couldn't read what he had written. He had been too sleepy to write neatly.

Neurons

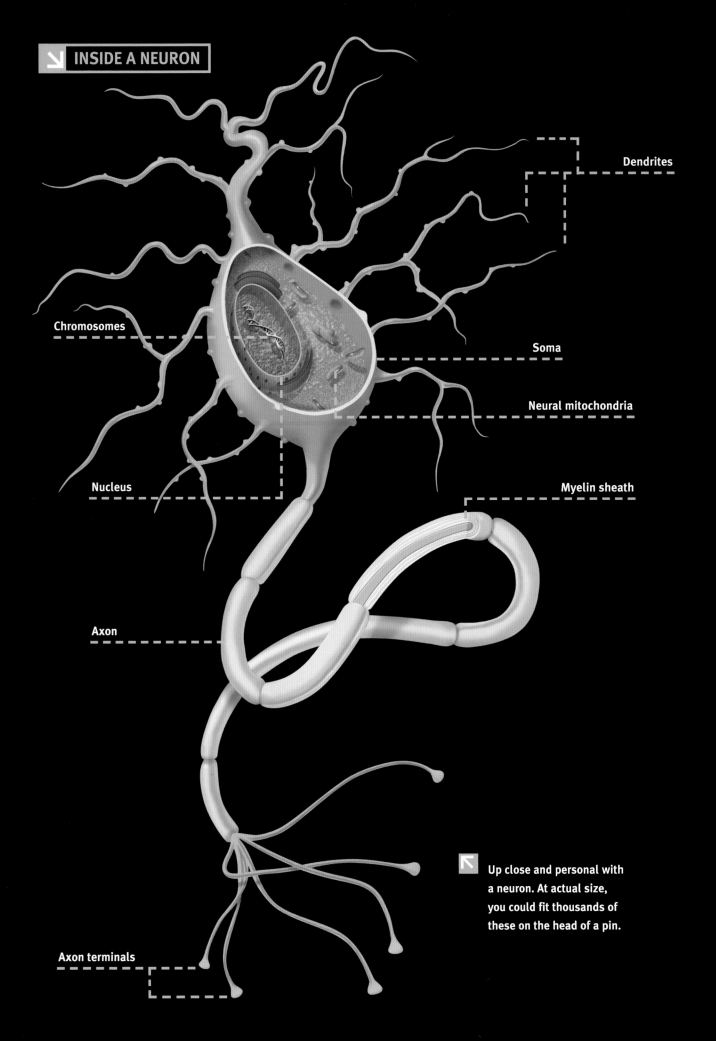

Dendrites

Chromosomes

Soma

Neural mitochondria

Nucleus

Myelin sheath

Axon

Axon terminals

Up close and personal with a neuron. At actual size, you could fit thousands of these on the head of a pin.

In yet another example of good luck in science, Loewi had the exact same dream the next night. This time, Loewi actually got up and went to his lab where he performed the experiment from his dream. First, he removed a heart from each of two frogs. He put the hearts in small vats filled with fluid and kept them beating by wiring them to a battery. He slowed down the first heart by triggering the correct nerve. Then he took the fluid from the first chamber and put it into the second chamber. Without changing the electricity, he observed that the second heart slowed down, too.

Loewi realized that the nerve in the first chamber must have released some "slow down" chemicals, and that those chemicals were floating around in the fluid. It turned out that Loewi was right: The brain works by using a combination of electricity and chemicals, which is called an electrochemical reaction.

STRUCTURE

Now you know that neurons are interesting-looking little cells that communicate using chemical reactions. But at their simplest, neurons are like tiny switches. Let's take a look at how neurons are structured; then we'll see how they work.

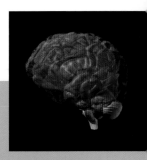

We'll start with the cell body. Called a soma, it is a lot like other cell bodies. A thin membrane holds it together. Inside, it has a nucleus, which contains chromosomes—as do all cell nuclei—and information about what the cell's particular job is. It also has a special kind of mitochondria—neural mitochondria—which produce energy for the cell. The mitochondria work hard because neurons live a long time. The other types of cells in your body die and are replaced on a regular basis—that's how you grow. But neurons are different. You have most of the same neurons throughout your life. They die over time, and they die faster as you get older. However, they aren't replaced. Once neurons die, they're gone.

Extending out from the back end of the soma is a long, whip-like attachment called an axon. There is usually only one axon attached to the soma, and it is incredibly thin—one hundred

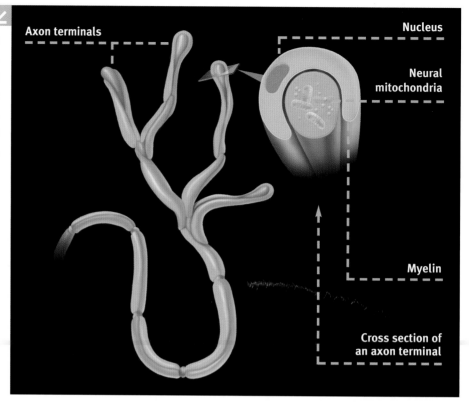

Axon terminals are like flattened pods. They contain neurotransmitters that will be blasted to the dendrites on other cells.

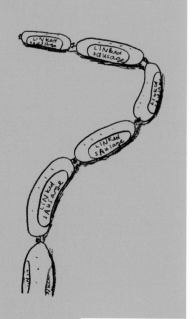

axons could easily fit next to one another across one strand of your hair. The axon is how the cell reaches out to the rest of the brain and to the central nervous system. It transmits the messages from the nucleus like a telephone wire. And like a telephone wire, the axon is protected from damage by a thin coating. This coating, called myelin, is made of shiny white fat. It is the substance that makes the brain's white matter appear white.

Myelin wraps the axon in sections that look like linked sausages. These sausage shapes extend out from where the axon leaves the soma to a group of fingerlike extensions called the axon terminals. Each of these terminals ends with what looks like a little flattened pad, almost like a tree frog's suction toes. These axon terminals store the chemicals that are used to communicate with other neurons. They stick out into the space between the neurons called the synapse.

On the other side of the synapse are dendrites of other neurons. These dendrites are the beginning, or front end, of every neuron. Dendrites look like wild, twisting, and spiky strands of hair on

Neurons

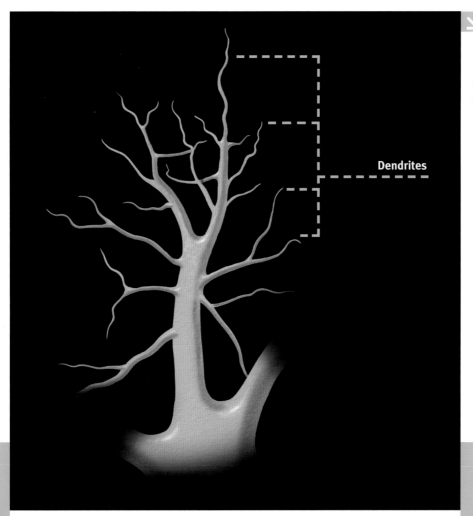

Dendrites

Dendrites extend in many directions, like tree branches or frizzy hair.

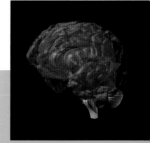

someone's head. They point in all different directions, and there may be hundreds of them on an individual neuron. The dendrites' job is to receive information from the axons of other neurons and bring it into their own neuron. Then the neuron passes that information along by its own axon, and that signal goes to the next neuron. This process goes on continuously in your brain—it never stops.

Because there are so many dendrites coming in and so many axon terminals going out, a single neuron may be connected to hundreds and even thousands of other cells—some of which might be in a completely different lobe of the brain. If you imagine that each of the one hundred billion neurons in your brain is connected to an average of one thousand other neurons, suddenly you have one hundred trillion (that's a 1 with fourteen zeros

Neurons

TYPES OF NEURONS

Almost all of the one hundred billion neurons in your body have the same structure: dendrites, a soma, and an axon. Yet there are many different types of neurons and they have different functions depending on where they are located. They have strange shapes (as in pyramidal and stellate neurons) and even strange names (like Purkinje cells), but their basic components are generally the same.

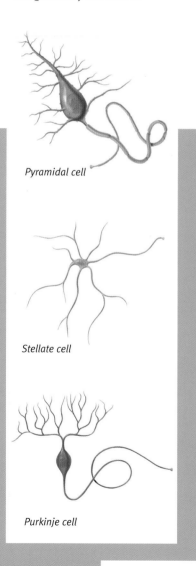

Pyramidal cell

Stellate cell

Purkinje cell

after it) different synaptic connections going on in your head every day of your entire life! Some scientists think the actual number of connections is far greater—perhaps as many as a quadrillion connections (that's a 1 with fifteen zeroes after it). That means there are more synapses in your head than there are grains of sand on any beach you've ever been to. It would take you thirty MILLION years just to count this high if you counted every single second of every single day.

The one hundred billion neurons inside your head stretch across your brain. But since they don't actually touch, how do they communicate with one another? That's where the chemical explosions come in. Let's go back to the nucleus in the middle of the soma and see how these explosions work. Imagine the nucleus is waiting for a signal from its dendrites. This waiting period—when the nucleus is "at rest"—lasts a mere fraction of a second. When a signal comes into the neuron from any of its hundreds of dendrites, a chemical reaction begins in the nucleus, much like what happens to a battery when you put it in a toy. Molecules in the nucleus become electrically charged and build up energy, like a miniature bomb waiting to go off. When the chemicals get charged up enough, they create a tiny blast—almost like a burp—that travels out into the axon. This "burp" is called the action potential or nerve impulse.

When this tiny blast occurs in the nucleus, the nerve impulse travels the length of the axon and enters the axon terminal. There, it hits neurotransmitter molecules stored in a pocket called a vesicle. As soon as the neurotransmitters are hit by the impulse, they blast out through the thin walls of the axon terminal. This process is called the "firing" of the synapse. The neurotransmitters fly across the synapse, like a skateboarder leaping between two ramps. It's not a long way, only about one millionth of an inch. When they cross the gap, the neurotransmitters smash into the dendrites of another neuron.

Now the information has been delivered to the dendrite of a new neuron. Dendrites have receptors that react when neurotransmit-

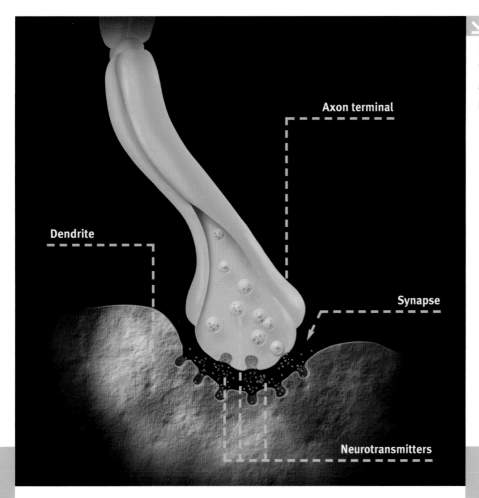

Axon terminal

Dendrite

Synapse

Neurotransmitters

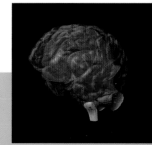

Neurotransmitters "jump the gap" like a skateboarder between two ramps.

ters hit them. Depending on the kind of neurotransmitter they receive, they send messages down their spiny lengths and into the soma, where the nucleus is at rest. The process starts all over again, as the nucleus in the next neuron takes the messages and creates its own electrical impulse. It spits that impulse down its axon and out across another synapse. This process happens hundreds of times per second, as each blast takes about one millisecond.

If the nucleus doesn't get the right kinds of signals from its dendrites, it won't fire. It's like a light switch, which is either on or off with no in-between. So even though the neuron is active, it may not be sending along signals. It is this decision—to pass along signals or not—that controls your movement, your thinking, your actions and reactions, and all of the other millions of things your brain is doing.

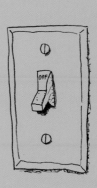

Neurons

SQUID NEURONS

In the past few years, scientists have learned a great deal about neurotransmitters. Much of the initial research on how neurotransmitters and electrochemical nerve activity takes place was done with a most unlikely animal—the squid. The squid has a big neuron that runs from its head to its tail. It is very wide by neuronal standards—about 1 millimeter. This means that it can be seen easily by scientists. They have used the squid neuron to test their theories of how neurons use electricity and chemicals. It has helped them to understand the actions that take place in human neurons.

Neurotransmitters that have been blasted across a synapse and smashed into the dendrites fall back into the space between the cells. They are then recycled. After they pass on their messages, they are pulled back into the vesicles in the axon terminal. Then they receive another message and leap the gap again, on and on, every split second of every hour of every day of your life.

When neurotransmitters are blasting, the process is called neuro-transmission. Neurotransmission is one of the most important things that occurs in your body because it is how the brain sends its messages.

There are lots of chemicals in the brain, but not all of the chemicals are neurotransmitters. In order for a chemical to be a neuro-transmitter, it has to be created in a neuron. Chemicals known as amino acids and peptides can be neurotransmitters if they fit this description. So far, science has identified about fifty different neu-rotransmitters, including dopamine (which contains information about movement and pleasure), serotonin (which contains infor-mation about wakefulness and sleepiness), bradykinin (which has information about pain), and epinephrine (which can speed up or slow down your body's various organs and systems).

NERVES AND THE BRAIN

Neurotransmission not only happens inside the brain, but also along the lengths of all the nerves in your body. Interestingly, all these messages travel down one-way streets. Just as the neuron takes in information from the dendrites and then whips it out the other end with the axon, nerve fibers go in only one direction. This means that one set of nerves brings information into the brain and a second set sends the information out of the brain.

The first set of nerves, the ones that bring sensory information into the brain, are called sensory nerves. The second set, those that send commands from the brain to the body, are called motor

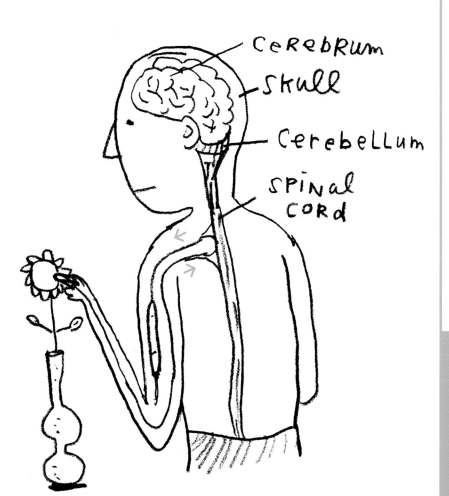

CEREBRUM
SKULL
CEREBELLUM
SPINAL CORD

One way in, another way out. Sensory and motor signals stay on their own paths when traveling between the brain and the body.

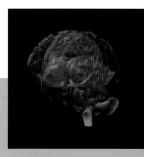

nerves. So if you're burning your fingers on a stove, the sensory nerves are sending information up to your brain about what's happening, and your brain is sending instructions down the motor nerves to tell your fingers to move. By using two different pathways, nerve signals can't bump into one another and get their messages confused.

Neurons

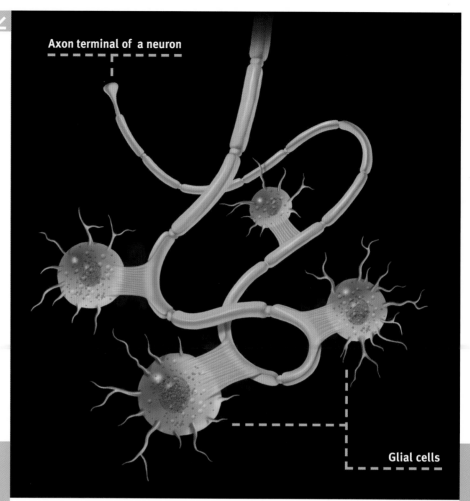

Axon terminal of a neuron

Glial cells

Glial cells attach to neurons and clean up after them— like janitors.

From everything we've talked about so far, it might sound like the entire brain—indeed, the entire central nervous system—is composed only of neurons. Certainly, neurons are the most important part of the brain. But these master communicators, the "higher-ups," need workers or laborers to help them. This is true in every organization, whether it's a beehive or a big company. And it's also true in the brain.

Because neurons are not packed in tightly with other neurons, they need help just staying in place. This job is done by little cells called glial cells. Glial cells serve a number of important purposes, mostly as caretakers of the brain. A group of glial cells is called glia. Glia means "glue," and much of what glia do is hold the neurons in place and protect them. There are many more glial cells than there are neurons—perhaps ten times as many. The myelin sheath that fits around axons is created by glial cells. This sheath protects the axon and makes sure that its signals don't get interrupted by other nearby axons (which would be a perfect example of "getting your wires crossed"). Glia also provide the nutrients for neurons by bringing in glucose and oxygen from the blood.

Glial cells have another important job: They are the brain's janitors. When neurons die, the glial cells break them down and move them out of the brain so they can be disposed of. And scientists have found evidence that glia can mop up neurotransmitters that may not have found their way back into the neuron's vesicles. This keeps those neurotransmitters from floating around in the brain and wandering into places they don't belong.

Working together, glia, neurons, and neurotransmitters act like one big machine with billions of parts—more than any machine ever made in a factory. But like any machine, if one part doesn't do its job, the brain stops working and shuts down. In order to keep this from happening, you have to take care of your brain. And there are ways that you can make your brain a better machine, as we'll see in the next chapter.

The care and Feeding of your Brain

You've seen what your brain is. You know what it's made of, how it's connected to the rest of your body, and how different parts of the brain control different parts of your body. ↗

6 THE CARE AND FEEDING OF YOUR BRAIN

CHAPTER SIX

You know that the left brain controls the right side of the body, and vice versa. You know about neurons and neurotransmitters. You know a lot about the brain.

One big mystery remains. How does the brain think? And how does it learn?

These are excellent questions. But we don't have all the answers yet. For many years, scientists described the brain as having two distinct functions.

The first function is referred to as the "mechanical brain," which controls your body's functions. It balances you when you walk and moves your arm when you throw a ball.

The second function of the brain is called "the mind," which is your thought center. It's where you learn math, draw pictures, write stories, think about what you want to be when you grow up—all the things animals don't do. The mind is involved in the things that help make us human.

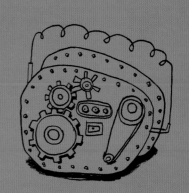

For hundreds of years, people have argued about where the mind actually is. Sure, we know where Broca's area and Wernicke's area are, and those are important in helping us understand the brain. But what part of our brain knows that it is a brain, that we

Care and Feeding

think with it, and that it guides us through life? In other words, what makes your brain aware of itself? Your hand isn't aware of itself; it doesn't have its own mind. Neither does your foot, or your stomach. But your brain is aware of everything, including itself. The problem is that scientists can't find that one spot in the brain that controls thinking.

And it gets more complicated. We can't say that the words to your favorite song or the image of your best friend's face are stored in particular brain cells. We don't know exactly where memories are stored. Not only do we not know *where* they are stored, we aren't even sure *how* they're stored. How does a neuron, or a group of neurons, hold on to the words to "Happy Birthday"? We just don't know.

It might seem like there is very little you can do to influence how your brain behaves. After all, with hundreds of billions of neurons and trillions of synaptic connections and messages being sent every thousandth of a second, what could you possibly do for your brain that it's not already doing for itself?

Well, as a matter of fact, there is a lot you can do for your brain. You can improve your learning, improve your memory, and keep your brain supplied with energy. Some of these improvements involve good eating and exercise, and some involve using tricks. Let's take a look.

LEARNING AND MEMORY

Learning has a lot to do with repeating facts and figures, like learning your spelling words or math tables and memorizing rules. You've done your addition tables from one to ten so many times you can usually add any number from one to ten without stopping to think about it. This is due to the fact that the tables are stored in your long-term memory because you have repeated them so much.

You also learn from your reactions to particular situations—situations you may want to repeat or avoid in the future. The first time you had a candy bar, you probably realized that you'd like to have one again—and again and again. Anytime you saw a candy bar after that, you easily remembered that it tasted good.

On the other hand, the first time you stick your fingers into a rotating fan will probably also be the last time. It only takes once for us to remember an event that causes pain. That's a lesson we learn very quickly, which keeps us from hurting ourselves over and over again.

Scientists believe that learning is a way that our brain sorts experiences into memories so that we can get to the memories as fast as possible. Every time a memory is made or an activity is learned, it appears that a new connection is made between neurons. An axon terminal reaches out to a new set of dendrites. The more often you repeat an activity, the more connections that are made and the easier it is to retrieve the memory. If you've got a connection from one neuron to a thousand others, it's a lot better than being connected to only one other neuron. With fewer connections, it's harder to find the right memories.

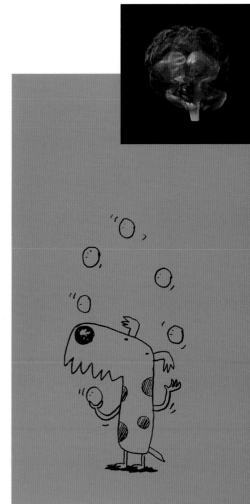

Researchers have found that it's important for babies to learn a lot when they're young because this is when the most neuronal connections are made. This is why babies can learn so fast. Listening to music and playing games with their hands helps babies make new connections between neurons. Many of your language connections were made when you were very young, which is why it's easier to learn new languages in grade school than when you're an older person. Older people's brains don't make connections as quickly or as often as young people's. That's why there's a saying "you can't teach an old dog new tricks." It's not necessarily true, but it is harder to get an older creature to learn new behaviors.

There is also some evidence that the ability to say certain things is hardwired in our brains as babies, especially certain sounds. Take the letter *R* for instance. Most English speakers find it hard to learn how to pronounce the rolling *R* used in French pronunciation. We often make it sound like *arrggh*. At the same time, many Asian speakers have difficulty with English *R* pronunciation, and will substitute a sound that is part *R* and part *L*. Even if adult speakers spend many years learning a new language, they may never get the *R* just right (the same thing applies to people from Eastern Europe, who will often replace *TH* sounds with a hard *Z* sound). It is thought that we can make these sounds only if the proper connections are made in our brains when we are young. Depending on where we live and the first language we learn, we may get one kind of connection but not another. If we learn many languages as children, we might get all of the pronunciations right. But after we become teenagers, it seems almost impossible to pronounce those sounds perfectly. The connections just don't get created anymore.

↘ RIGHT BRAIN VERSUS LEFT BRAIN

As you've probably figured out, learning is closely associated with memory. If we can keep a lot of memories in our head, we have more information to use when we're thinking or learning something new.

The way we think and learn, and what we think and learn, has a lot to do with the fact that our brain is divided in half. The left side of our brain is important for speech and language. It is also important for developing logic and mathematical skills. On the other side of the corpus callosum, the right brain is considered to be the creative brain. That's where our ability to play music or paint pictures or write books is developed. In most people, the two halves work together so that we are able to do lots of different things.

You might hear people referred to as "left brainers" or "right brainers." Left brainers are supposedly good scientists, accountants, and computer programmers. Right brainers are supposedly good artists and musicians, and are more involved in the design or development of things. It's as if the person who designs a skyscraper is the right-brain person, and the person who actually constructs it is the left-brain person. But we can't divide the world

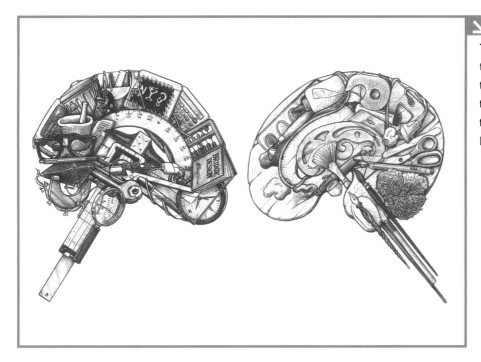

These drawings show the kinds of abilities that the left side of the brain (left) and the right side of the brain (right) control.

into right and left brainers. In reality, most people use a mixture of both sides of their brains.

It may be true, however, that some people who excel at math have managed to make more connections in their left brains than in their right. The same is true of painters and the right side of the brain. Isn't it interesting that you don't hear about a lot of painters who are great scientists? Or great mathematicians who are also great actors? Sometimes, a person really does seem to favor one side of the brain over the other.

TRAINING YOUR BRAIN

One way that some people believe you can strengthen your brain is by doing tasks that emphasize one side or the other. To do this, you try to trick one side into working harder than the other. There are a number of ways to do this; some are easy, some are hard.

• Try holding your fork or spoon in the other hand when you eat.
• Switch your watch to a different arm.
• When you're singing a song, change the words in the middle— just throw in whatever comes to mind.

Care and Feeding

MAKE UP YOUR OWN MNEMONICS

Make up a tune. Make up a nonsense story. I used a mnemonic for this book when I was writing about the meninges. In order to remember the names and the order of the three meninges layers, I used the word PAD. First of all, the meninges is a pad for the brain, but it also contains the first letter of each layer—in order from inside out. Pia mater, Arachnoid layer, and Dura mater. PAD. It worked for me every time.

Mnemonics don't have to make sense. When I first moved to New York City, it was easy to remember most streets because they were numbered. But downtown, some of the streets aren't numbered—they have names instead—and they are hard to tell apart. They are Bleecker, Houston, Prince, Spring, and Canal. So that I wouldn't miss my subway stops on these streets, I made up a sentence that contained the streets in order. "In Bleecker Houston, the Prince Springs over the Canal." I always remember Houston on a foggy day with a little prince jumping over a canal of water. It might not make a lot of sense, but I never miss my subway stop.

- Draw pictures without looking at the paper.
- Try to recite the alphabet backward.
- Count to one hundred by threes.

When you change the way you do these tasks, you force your brain to work in ways it hasn't before. It has to learn how to do these things a new way, which means more neuron connections get made.

And while no one can guarantee that learning new ways of doing things will make your brain stronger, it certainly adds new experiences, which are stored as new information in your memory.

There are many tricks you can use to improve your memory. Can't remember a person's name? Quickly run through the alphabet, one letter at a time, and see if that helps. Like Adam, Arnold, Bob, Bill, Bert, and so on. Can't remember where you left something? Go back one activity at a time in your mind until you get to the point where you saw it last. Or if you lost it a long time ago, try to remember how it looked the last time you saw it, where it was lying, and what was around it. Remembering the environment can help trigger memories.

Mnemonics

How can you trick your brain on purpose? Well, you've been doing it your whole life.

Because language is a vital part of being human, many brain tricks are based on using language in a fun or familiar way. One of the most useful and common language tricks we use to remember things is called mnemonics. Mnemonics are devices (a nice word for tricks) that people use to improve their memory. These can be little sayings or nonsense rhymes that help you remember things in a particular order or in some special arrangement, or even to remember simple things like names, numbers, or streets.

One popular mnemonic is the rule for spelling: "*I* before *E,* except after *C.*" This will help you to better remember how to spell "piece" and "receive." Another one is designed to help you remember the musical lines and spaces on a staff: The lines E, G, B, D, and F become "Every Good Boy Deserves Fudge." The spaces F, A, C, E become the word "FACE."

Your brain can interpret millions of different shades across the seven colors of the spectrum. It's easy to remember those seven basic colors in order when you turn their first letters into a man's name: Roy G. Biv. That stands for red, orange, yellow, green, blue, indigo, and violet.

Memory Tricks

Perhaps the most obvious device—and all of us have done it—is when you learned your ABCs. You probably learned the ABCs as a song, the one that has the same tune as "Twinkle, Twinkle, Little Star" and "Baa Baa Black Sheep." If you recite your ABCs right now, you'll probably say them in a singsongy way.

What you did by learning the ABCs this way was create several kinds of connections for your brain: One connection learned the letters, another remembered the music, and yet another linked them together. By using music, which is often stored in long-term memory by the hippocampus, you made your brain hold on to the ABCs faster and longer than it might have if you just tried to learn the twenty-six different letters that had no obvious—or easy-to-remember—connections. That would seem almost impossible, wouldn't it? To prove it, try to say the ABCs backward. They're the same letters, and you're just reversing the order, but it's almost impossible to do. We've never made the brain connections that help us to recite these very familiar letters in a different order.

Memory Palace

Memory tricks can get more and more complicated depending on what you want to remember. One memory trick is actually an elaborate device called a memory palace. It's a tough trick, but it works

The concept of a memory palace was first put forth by the Greek poet Simonides, who lived around 500 BC. One afternoon, he was hired to read a poem to a huge crowd assembled in a banquet hall. Later that evening, the banquet hall caved in and killed all the guests—smashing them up so much they couldn't be identified. Simonides was brought back to the room. By remembering how each table looked as he read his poem, he could remember who was sitting at each table.

People expanded on Simonides's idea of remembering what was in the banquet room and built bigger palaces to keep their memories. Some people have created memory palaces throughout their lives that have hundreds of rooms. An Italian priest named Matteo Ricci was one of those people. In the 1500s, he earned the respect of Chinese scholars by teaching them how to build memory palaces. China's culture required that its scholars remember many things, from laws and ceremonies to stories and lectures. Ricci showed them how to use the country's grand palaces as models for imaginary palaces where they could store their memories.

with practice. In a memory palace, you create an imaginary palace (it can even be modeled on your own home) and place things you want to remember in that palace. But first you create rooms in that imaginary palace to store things. So if you need to remember the names of certain books, imagine putting a book in each room. Then when you go back to each room, try to remember which book was in there. Looking at the room, and its colors, may help you remember the book. As time goes on, you might be able to add more things to each room. That way, you build up little memory rooms that store the things you need to remember. Eventually, you can create an entire palace.

There is one very important thing to keep in mind while you're trying these different memory tricks. The fact that your memory can be tricked also means that sometimes your memory itself is not perfect. This may happen because pieces of memories come from different parts of your brain—the images, the sounds, the smells, and so on. Your brain has to actually reassemble the pieces into one memory. The pieces might not always add up in the right way.

You also run into this same type of "reassembled" memory problem when two or more people tell their sides of a story. Each person may have a different version of events, and each will insist that they remember it correctly. In fact, each of their memories may have made a slight change to the story when the brain was rebuilding it so that no version is perfectly accurate. It's possible that the longer we go without calling up particular memories (such as events when you were younger), the harder they become to remember—or rebuild—correctly.

THE THINKING BRAIN VERSUS THE EMOTIONAL BRAIN

Fear

Even the easiest task becomes difficult when you are scared or nervous. This is because when you are scared your limbic system is trying to control your thinking brain. The fear factor makes simple things hard to do: hitting a baseball when the winning run is up to you, riding a bicycle as huge trucks roar loudly by, or having to finish an important exam before the time is up.

Think about what you're afraid of—and why. Are you afraid of snakes? Spiders? Taking tests? Skiing? Climbing? Raising your hand in class? Are your friends afraid of the same things? Figuring out what you're afraid of, and then using your thinking brain to determine if it can hurt you or not, might help you stop being afraid of it.

What do you think most people are afraid of? Usually, people are afraid of things that can hurt them, like firecrackers or wild animals or falling from a high place. They are also afraid of doing things that might get them into trouble. But do you know the number-one thing that most people fear? Speaking in public. It may be hard to believe, but people are generally more afraid of talking in front of a group or a classroom than they are of snakes, lions, flying in airplanes, or going to jail.

Why is this? After all, public speaking isn't dangerous; it can't physically hurt you. The reason it's so scary to so many people is because of a weird reversal of the way things in our brain normally work. In the case of making a speech, the thinking brain makes its fears more important than the fears controlled by the limbic system, our emotional brain. Remember that our "fight or flight" and fear centers are located in the limbic system.

You could agree that public speaking isn't a dangerous situation, but your thinking brain might disagree. It worries about being embarrassed, or being made fun of, or making a big mistake. These feelings are made much worse when your thinking brain realizes that lots of other people are watching you. It knows that you have to live with a feeling of embarrassment if you make a big mistake in front of a crowd. Your thinking brain doesn't want to have this feeling, or this memory, and so it creates a fear of public speaking.

The thinking brain can make us afraid of things that can't hurt us, yet it can also do the opposite: It can teach us to not be afraid of

Way down on the street, one hundred thousand people watched twenty-four-year-old Petit perform his daring walk.

There are some fears that we may never get over, no matter how much we think about them. It is unlikely that you would be willing to stand on the edge of a 100-story skyscraper and look down, at least not without something to hold on to. Even then, most people would be too scared to do this because with one tiny slip, they'd be falling a very long way.

That's a scary thing to imagine, but let's make it even scarier. What if you were asked to walk out on a tightrope attached to the tops of two skyscrapers? The wire would hang far above the city with other buildings and the street far below—and there wouldn't be anything to hold on to. No amount of money, no amount of threats, and no amount of pleading would ever get you to walk on a tightrope up that high. But one man, Philippe Petit, did just that. Philippe is a tightrope walker who has been doing very dramatic performances for many years. He has walked on tightropes all over the world, from Australia to Europe.

On August 7, 1974, Philippe walked on a wire between the World Trade Center towers in New York City. The buildings were 100 feet apart, and the wire was strung from one building to the other. He walked across the tightrope more than 1,000 feet in the air. There was no net, no safety ropes, nothing to hang on to. Just Philippe and a balancing pole.

Philippe didn't walk between the buildings just once, he walked back and forth eight times. He even stopped a few times to sit on the wire. And Philippe wasn't scared. He had convinced himself he could do it. For one thing, he knew that his body had excellent balance. For another thing, his brain knew that if he could walk perfectly across a wire a few feet in the air—which he did all the time—then he could walk across a wire almost one-quarter of a mile in the air.

Guess how long it took him to prepare for this huge event so that his brain would be able to tell his body to walk across the wire? Five years.

things that really are scary or dangerous. While many of us would never walk into a burning building, firefighters do it every day. Many of us would be afraid of fighting in a war, yet millions of people have done that since the beginning of time. You might be afraid to parachute, scuba dive, or go rock climbing. That's understandable; these activities are all risky, and if something goes wrong, you *could* get hurt. That's a natural fear. Yet at this very moment, people all over the world are parachuting, scuba diving, and rock climbing—and they're having a fun time doing it.

Some people who like to do risky things may have never been afraid of these activities. Other people might have decided to give the risky activity a try and found that it wasn't scary after all. It's like riding a roller coaster or watching a horror movie; it looks incredibly scary at the beginning, but by the time it's over, you know that everything is okay. Realizing this can get rid of the initial fear forever.

Phobias

Extreme fear of something is called a phobia. There are hundreds of phobias. Some are easy to understand, such as fear of fire, tornadoes, or disease. After all, these things can hurt or kill you. Then there are unusual phobias that might seem silly to you, but are very real to those people who have them. These include phobias like fear of clowns, fear of sunlight, or fear of the number 13. In the case of these unusual phobias, an event may have occurred early in a person's life to make them afraid of certain things. As they grew up, their particular fears got worse.

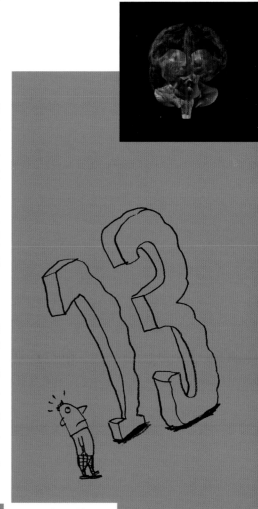

Many phobias can be cured by doctors who help patients realize that what they are scared of can't really hurt them. It takes a lot of time because the thinking brain has to unlearn a fear that it has created. Oftentimes, the fear has to be confronted directly: A person who is afraid of flying is taken on a short plane ride to see how safe it is, or someone who is afraid of a particular kind of animal may visit a zoo with an animal trainer to see that the animal isn't scary.

Care and Feeding

Intelligence

One of the most difficult things to measure about the brain is how smart it is or, in other words, how smart you are. The tests you take in school aren't indications of how smart you are, or how smart you might be in other subjects. They generally show how well you have learned a particular lesson or how well you memorized a set of words or numbers. Intelligence is the ability to learn or understand or deal with new or unexpected situations. It is how you respond to or utilize your environment.

About one hundred years ago, during the early 1900s, the idea of measuring a person's smartness—or intelligence quotient (IQ)—became very popular. This was also the time when people began to discuss evolution, brain development, and the origins of individual personality.

A number of researchers came up with different tests to identify how smart people were. The first popular IQ test was created in 1916 and was called the Stanford-Binet test. It is still used today. The questions on the Stanford-Binet test ask about many different things that most people are expected to know, especially some obvious things about the world. Much of it examines your language abilities.

Your score on the Stanford-Binet test takes into account whether you answered the question correctly and how old you are. Your score is compared to the scores of other people your age. The average person has an IQ of about 100. Someone who has a score of more than 140 is considered a genius. A score of less than 70 indicates possible mental retardation, while a score of 40 and under shows that a person may be severely retarded and may not be able to do even the simplest tasks by themselves.

The more we find out about the brain, though, the less people believe IQ tests are an accurate measure of how smart we are. Some people are good at book learning, but may not be very good at learning from their experiences. Other people aren't good at taking written tests, but may be very good at answering questions out loud. Intelligence quotient tests may give a general idea of what people know or how they figure things out, but these tests can't really tell with certainty how smart someone is. Still, until something better comes along, you'll probably hear people mention IQ tests during your life.

↘ SLEEP

We spend about eight hours a day sleeping, which is one-third of each twenty-four-hour day. Over the years, this adds up to a lot of time. By the time you turn twenty-one, you will already have slept a total of seven years. If sleep weren't so important, your body wouldn't be doing so much of it.

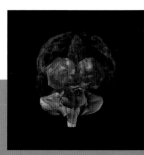

All animals sleep. We think of sleep as a time when creatures can rest their bodies after a day of running around and hunting for food or going to school and playing sports. But taking a break from physical activity is only a small part of the benefits of sleep. People who sit at office desks all day need as much sleep as more active people. This is because sleep is essential to the brain's health. It's a lot like plugging in a video camera at night to recharge it after the batteries have been worn down during the day.

As far as we know, sleep gives your brain a chance to focus on the needs of your body without the distraction of the outside world. While you sleep, your body slows down, giving your heart, lungs, and other organs a rest after a busy day. The brain also releases more growth hormones at night. Growth hormones are the chemicals that instruct all the parts of your body, from your hair to your fingers, to keep growing. And your brain can use the time to work on repairing or replacing damaged or dying cells.

Sleep is also important when you're sick because it gives your brain and your body a chance to fight illness without having to worry about what's going on in the outside world. It's hard to get better when you're running around at school, trying to concentrate on a test, or going to softball practice. Your brain needs to

Care and Feeding

focus on mending, and too many interruptions slow down the healing process.

Stages of Sleep

You have different types, or stages, of sleep every night. While you sleep, your brain goes on a roller-coaster ride through these different stages. Each stage or cycle can be measured by an electroencephalograph (EEG), a machine that measures electrical activity in the brain.

The first stage (think of it as the top of the roller-coaster ride) is when you lose contact with the world around you just as you fall asleep. The second stage, as you begin to slide down the roller-coaster ride, sends you into light sleep, separating your brain even more from the outside world. At this stage, you can still be easily awakened.

In stage three, you hit deep sleep, and most of your body functions have slowed down significantly. If someone whispers to you, you probably won't hear them. Finally, you drop into stage-four sleep. Stage four is the bottom of the roller-coaster drop, and it's as far from being awake as your brain can be. It's the deepest stage of sleep. It's very difficult for someone to wake you up when you're in stage-four sleep. This is the level where you're "dead to the world," and almost nothing outside your body can get through to your brain without being very loud, very rough, or very bright.

Stages one through four are called slow-wave sleep. This is because the activity in your brain is generating waves that move very slowly.

After you've spent about an hour going from stage one to stage four, your brain starts going back up the next slope of the roller coaster. You go from stage four back up to three, and then to two. But before you get to stage one and start to wake up, your body does something very strange. The pons in your brain stem starts sending out nerve impulses, and your brain tells different parts of your body to speed

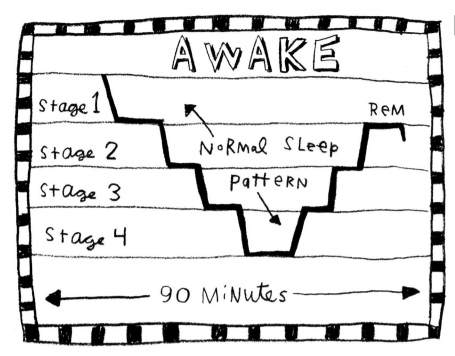

This 90-minute normal sleep cycle is repeated about five times each night.

up. Your heartbeat increases. Your eyes start moving around, as if you were looking at things like you do when you're awake. But your eyes are still closed, and you're still asleep. We call this period rapid eye movement, or REM for short.

At this point in your sleep cycle, your brain is very active, almost as if it is awake. This is your dream period, and it lasts from about five to fifteen minutes.

After this burst of mental activity—your body may even twitch during REM sleep—your brain starts dropping from REM sleep back down through stage two, stage three, to stage four sleep again. This cycle of going up and down on the sleep roller coaster happens about five times a night (depending on how long you sleep). Each cycle lasts about ninety minutes.

Dreams

While sleep is great for helping your body recover from a long day or from an illness, the most important part of sleep may be dreaming. This is when the brain has a chance to sort, categorize,

Care and Feeding

115

↘ Peter Tripp's charity event turned into a nightmare when he could no longer tell the difference between reality and his sleep-deprived imagination.

One of the best examples of what can happen to someone who doesn't get any dream time was Peter Tripp, a radio disc jockey. Back on January 21, 1959, Tripp agreed to stay awake on the radio for at least two hundred hours—more than eight days—as part of a "wake-a-thon" that would raise money for charity.

After staying awake through the first few days without too much trouble, Tripp's mental abilities soon started to go out of control. By his fourth day of sleeplessness, Tripp couldn't concentrate. He also began to hallucinate; he saw spiders everywhere. He was convinced that his shoes were coated with spiderwebs.

What was happening was that Tripp's brain was demanding sleep and trying to reset itself. Because he wouldn't go to sleep, his brain might have been creating REM states even though he was awake.

As the days progressed, Tripp saw other animals, like rabbits and kittens, running around his room. He claimed that a man who came to visit him was wearing a suit of worms. He spent long periods of time looking for money in empty desk drawers. He also began to act nasty toward his friends, and thought they were trying to do things to hurt him.

When a doctor came to examine him toward the end of the stunt, Tripp thought the doctor was an undertaker who had come to bury him alive. Finally, Tripp couldn't take it anymore, and at two hundred and one hours, ten minutes, he called it quits. He then went to bed and slept for thirteen hours. When he woke up, he claimed to feel fine and refreshed. His brain appeared to have reset itself with no problem.

and sift through what it has encountered during the day. Most people have dreams during four or five different periods each night. While you're dreaming, your brain creates imaginary situations—even imaginary worlds. Interestingly, dreaming only occurs during particular times when you're asleep.

Scientists are not sure why we dream. One theory is that your brain uses dreams to classify certain memories that didn't get sorted when you were awake. The brain uses this time to put some in long-term memory and erase others as useless short-term memories. Perhaps some memories haven't been put in their proper place, so they're lying around like scraps of paper on your brain's floor. As the brain picks up these pieces, it tries to make sense out of them and pieces them together into dreams as if they were stories. Because the pieces aren't necessarily related, the dreams might not make sense to us when we think about them after we wake up. (It's as if everyone in your class brought in pieces of their home videos and you tried to make them all into one video that made sense.)

Another theory is that dreaming gives the brain a chance to reset itself to a "starting" position for the day to come. Like a Rubik's Cube that starts out with all the colors perfectly grouped together on each side, the brain might start each morning in perfect order, ready to go. But dealing with new situations and new experiences means that the brain has to make adjustments during the day. At the end of the day, the brain has done so much work that experiences, memories, images, and sounds are scattered every which way—just like a mixed-up Rubik's Cube. Dreams may be a way for your brain to move all of these elements back into place by putting everything where it belongs.

Your brain needs to dream to settle down and sort through certain things—memories, events, thoughts—in order to keep itself healthy and in working order. We know that mammals dream, or at least they experience REM sleep. You might have seen this when a sleeping dog growls or starts moving its paws, or a cat meows in its sleep. These are signs that the animal is dreaming.

Care and Feeding

On the other hand, reptiles and fish probably don't need to dream because their brains are essentially relying only on instinct to get them through the day. They don't need to do any thinking about events that occur around them day to day.

Scientists have learned a great deal about animal brains and dreaming by studying the echidna, also known as the spiny anteater. The echidna is an egg-laying mammal (like a platypus) that is native to Australia. And sometime during its development, perhaps millions of years ago, its brain might have been trapped between the worlds of reptiles and mammals.

The echidna goes through slow-wave sleep, stages one through four, but apparently never goes into REM sleep. Scientists know this because they took EEG readings of sleeping echidnas. What makes the echidna really interesting, though, is that its brain is exceptionally large compared to other animals of its size. Its cortex, where thinking occurs, makes up fifty percent of its brain. Even though it has such a big brain, the echidna doesn't have any REM sleep, which means it probably doesn't dream. Scientists think that all of the things an echidna learns or experiences during the day may not get sorted or removed while the echidna sleeps. The echidna's cortex might have to be so big because it has to store all of the echidna's memories. Its brain may be like a warehouse that can't be cleaned out.

The echidna's inability to dream, along with its big brain, seems to support the idea that brains need to be cleaned out. This seems especially true in humans, who probably use REM sleep to clear their brains of unwanted information.

Getting REM sleep is important to keep our brains in good working order. Not getting enough REM sleep can be a very nasty thing. Without REM sleep, your brain has to do its sorting and cleaning while you are awake. This can cause hallucinations that you might think are real, which can be very frightening. For this reason, keeping people awake has been used as a form of torture for hundreds of years. (Legend has it that two thousand years ago, the

If I could only dream.

The echidna can't use any of its big brain for daydreaming. In fact, it can't dream at all.

Romans killed their enemy, King Perseus of Macedonia, by not letting him fall asleep.) Tests in laboratories have shown that people regularly hallucinate if they aren't allowed to go into REM sleep. And there is a strange disease that affects several families in Italy, in which people eventually die from not being able to fall asleep. This disease, called fatal familial insomnia, is extremely rare, and makes people stay awake for weeks and weeks until their brains and their bodies give up.

The important thing to remember is that a good night's sleep seems to make up for REM sleep that has been missed or skipped. The brain brings itself all the way back to normal, usually in just one night. This means that even a little REM sleep is better than none at all. And sleep gives your brain a chance to focus on the needs of your body, repairing damaged skin, growing more hair, and rebuilding your strength without interruption. So you can help keep your brain healthy by making sure to keep it rested.

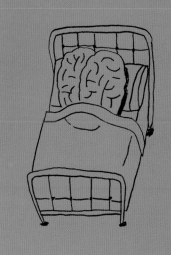

Care and Feeding

TREATING THE BRAIN . . . WHICH CAN BE A BIT GHASTLY AT TIMES

Some of the most unusual problems that affect humans are problems that occur in the brain. ↗

7 Treating the Brain...
WHICH can be a BiT
ghastly at Times

CHAPTER SEVEN

Over the course of history, in order to deal with brain problems, medical science has constructed some very strange cures. Some of the cures are pretty gruesome by modern standards.

As you've learned, the earliest surgeries may have been the trepanning of skulls five thousand years ago by primitive tribes to relieve headaches or release evil spirits. Metal tools and sharp rocks were used to open holes in the heads of living patients. How long these patients lived after their operations is not known. Without anesthesia or clean operating rooms, though, they probably didn't enjoy the experience at all—no matter how long they lived.

The tools used in brain surgery improved over the centuries, but the reasons for operating were the same as they had been. Operations were performed on people who had awful headaches, who behaved strangely, who had tumors that pushed out of the skulls, and on those who had bashed-in skulls.

There are stories of people having brain surgery during the Middle Ages—between AD 500 and 1500—to treat falling sickness (epilepsy) and madness (insanity). The fact that the brain was operated on for these conditions was only a coincidence because people didn't know that the brain had anything to do with

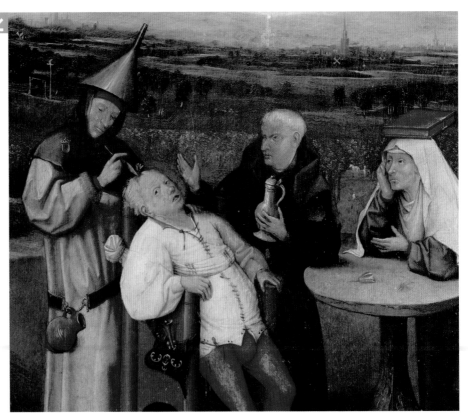

Hieronymus Bosch painted this scene of barbers performing brain surgery to remove the "stone of madness."

epilepsy or insanity. So how did they know that they should be operating on the brain at all?

Believe it or not, these operations were the result of barbers trying to make money. Yes, barbers. During the Middle Ages (also called the Dark Ages, in part because people weren't very educated), barbers were taught how to be surgeons for two reasons. One was that barbers knew how to use razors, which was important if you had to operate on someone. The other reason was that many of the real surgeons had died from a disease called the Black Death, or the Plague, which killed a huge part of the population of Europe. That gave barbers the chance to "play doctor" for real.

A not-very-honest group of these barber-surgeons, sometimes called "flying barbers," would visit a town for a few days, offering to cure people of anything that made them sick or feel bad. These barbers claimed that what made people act strangely was an imaginary "stone of madness" that was located in the head. According to the barbers, removing the stone would help the problem. Of course, they wanted money for this service. The barbers would then operate on people and take out bits of brain, claiming that these were pieces of the stone of madness.

Even though these barbers were fake doctors, the amazing thing is that they were probably helping some people with severe conditions without even knowing it. Removing small sections of the brain can help people who have certain types of brain disease or disorders. (For instance, modern surgeons will remove parts of the temporal lobe to stop epileptic seizures.) The barbers who lived during the Middle Ages are another part of the curious history of accidents and coincidences that contributed to understanding the brain.

It wasn't until about the 1800s that scientists realized how important the brain was to the body. With discoveries like those made by Paul Broca, and the surgeries performed by William Macewen, a whole new way of treating the brain came about. From that point forward, scientists and doctors gave the brain more respect and, in most cases, worked to develop effective ways to help patients with brain conditions.

Surgery became important in treating both physical damage to the brain and behavioral problems. One thing neuroscientists had figured out—and Phineas Gage contributed to this knowledge—was that certain behaviors could be affected by destroying or removing parts of the brain. If Gage, a normal man, had become violent, they wondered, then couldn't violent men become normal by removing a different part of the brain? Scientists began experimenting on animals to see if it was possible. The initial tests were done to make vicious animals, like wild dogs, tamer and more controllable. Researchers found that removing the temporal lobes of dogs calmed the animals down and made them gentle.

Other researchers at Yale were doing experiments with the brains of chimpanzees. These researchers found that if the apes had their frontal lobes removed—in a procedure called a lobotomy— they would become less aggressive. More important, after the operations, the chimpanzees still retained all their other abilities and their intelligence.

In 1892, a Swiss doctor named Gottlieb Burkhardt decided to try this procedure on humans. He was the director of a mental institution and had six violent patients that he thought might be helped by removing parts of their brains. Burkhardt drilled holes in each of their heads and removed various parts of their lobes. After the operations, four of the patients did indeed become less violent, so his process seemed to have worked. However, he never got the chance to test the other two—they died from their operations.

The scientific community was not impressed with Burkhardt's work, claiming it was inhuman. They demanded that no other doctors do this kind of drastic surgery. And no one did—for a while.

In the 1930s, Antonio Egas Moniz, a Portuguese doctor, combined the findings of the Yale researchers with those of Gottlieb Burkhardt. He thought that violent tendencies probably resulted from improper connections between the frontal lobe and the rest of the brain, especially the thalamus. He believed the bad connections were the cause of psychosis, a disorder in which people can't function normally because of abnormal fears or behaviors. Moniz guessed that if he could separate the frontal lobe from the midbrain, he might help people who had these kinds of problems.

Moniz then drilled a hole in each side of a patient's head and, using a wire knife called a leukotome, sliced through the brain on one side and then the other. The procedure, called a leukotomy, was dangerous, long, and not always successful. Like Burkhardt before him, Moniz was destined to be forgotten for doing something that sorta-kinda-maybe worked.

And then Walter Freeman came along. Freeman, an American neurologist, believed that Moniz had the right idea. In 1945, he developed a procedure called the prefrontal lobotomy. It was done by jabbing an ice pick into an eye socket. It became wildly popular.

Lobotomies weren't the only way to treat mental illness during the mid-1900s. Another "cure" was called electroconvulsive therapy, more commonly known as electroshock. This procedure is performed by strapping the patient onto a table, attaching electrodes to the patient's head, and blasting electricity through his or her brain. The electrical jolt creates a strong convulsion that is similar to what happens during an epileptic seizure. For some reason, it seemed to make people less violent and hyperactive, but only for short periods of time. The process had to be repeated again and again; eventually, patients suffered new problems from all the shocks. Electroshock was popular for a long time, but its use died out like lobotomies did. Interestingly, there are limited uses for electroshock today, but those uses are much more specific than they were fifty years ago.

During the time of Burkhardt's research, Harvey Cushing, an American doctor who taught at Yale University, was establishing the best ways to remove tumors from the brain. He was the first neurosurgeon to use X-rays to find the location of brain tumors, and he invented many procedures for use in brain surgery. By the time he died in 1939, Harvey Cushing was known as the "father of neurosurgery."

In the 1950s and 1960s, medications and surgeries designed to treat specific illnesses gradually replaced all these gruesome remedies. As scientists learned more about the brain, they learned how to make drugs affect specific parts of it. Treatment with drugs is much more effective—and less harmful—than hammering an ice pick into an eye socket or shocking people into having fits.

Brain surgery is still done to repair many things that affect the brain, from aneurysms to hydrocephalus. Today, neurosurgeons use computers to map out their surgical procedures down to the millimeter. Brain scans of different types—MRI, PET, MEG—help

Treating the Brain

Walter Freeman was fond of getting his picture in newspapers and medical journals. Freeman, who was not a surgeon, started recommending leukotomies for use in American mental institutions, claiming that the process would take care of the many severe disorders encountered in asylums. The only problem from Freeman's point of view was that the procedure took too long and was rather messy, since you had to drill two holes in the head to get into the brain.

Plus, Freeman couldn't perform a leukotomy by himself because he wasn't a surgeon. So in 1945 he came up with a procedure that would speed up the operation—and could be done by anybody.

All it took was an ice pick, which is like a pointed screwdriver, and a hammer—two items he could buy in a hardware store. Freeman gave his patient some local anesthesia so that what was about to happen wouldn't be too painful. He would slip the ice pick into an eye socket, just between the eyeball and the bridge of the nose. Then with a hammer, he would pound the pick through the bony eye socket, shattering it. The ice pick would pierce through the meninges and stab into the brain. Grabbing the handle of the pick, Freeman would then wiggle it around—hard—so that it slashed up the front of the brain. After a few moments, he would pull the pick out of the patient's head. The connections between the frontal lobe and the thalamus were cut. The operation was done. This procedure became one of the most popular, though gruesome, types of brain surgery ever invented.

How did Freeman come up with the idea of using an ice pick? Because all the normal surgical tools made at that time kept snapping off inside people's heads.

If this sounds incredibly gross, it was. Other doctors reportedly fainted when they watched this operation. But it seemed to work, and suddenly Freeman's lobotomies were being performed all over the world.

Part of the reason for their popularity was due to the end of World War II. Many people who had gone to war had suffered severe depression, nervous breakdowns, or other mental illness. Many soldiers were committed to mental hospitals in the late 1940s, and those institutions were overcrowded. Doctors at mental hospitals didn't know what to do with so many patients.

Under these circumstances, lobotomies with an ice pick and a hammer seemed like a quick and easy way to handle the problem. Plus, they were cheap. The cost for an ice-pick lobotomy was two hundred and fifty dollars; the cost for treating an inmate at an asylum was thirty-five thousand dollars a year. Nearly twenty thousand lobotomies were performed in the United States during the 1940s, and thousands more were done in other countries. The surgery was done to treat almost any problem that seemed to involve the brain. President John F. Kennedy's sister Rosemary was given a lobotomy as treatment for her mild retardation. A famous actress named Frances Farmer was forced to have one after her family and movie studio bosses decided she was getting too difficult to work with. She wasn't mentally ill, but her family hoped the operation would make her easier to get along with. It did, but she never starred in a movie again.

After rushing to perform lobotomies, doctors started examining exactly what all these surgeries had accomplished. They found that the surgeries hadn't accomplished much. Only about a third of the people got better, and that

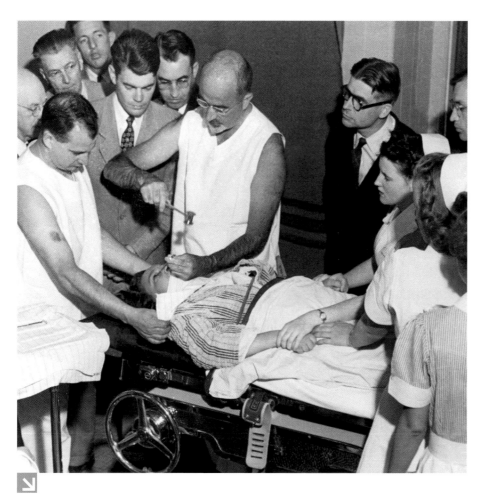

↘
Lobotomies were easy to perform, but gruesome to watch. Observers sometimes fainted once the hammering started.

was the same number who would have gotten better using other types of treatment. Many patients actually got worse, and many of them died. Suddenly, lobotomies didn't look so good after all.

The ice pick was eventually put away, although it is occasionally used in some countries. The book and movie *One Flew Over the Cuckoo's Nest* examined the use of ice-pick lobotomies as a way to quiet down loud patients in a mental hospital. Fortunately, the movie is the closest that people today will get to experiencing a lobotomy.

Treating the Brain

neurosurgeons take a look at the condition of the brain before they go to work.

When a neurosurgeon cuts into the skull to get to the brain, the procedure is called a craniotomy. Craniotomy means cutting the cranium, and it is done with a specialized saw called a craniotome. Except for the craniotomy, modern brain surgery does not usually involve knives or scalpels. Brain tissue is too soft to cut with a scalpel (try to remove pieces of Jell-O from your plate with a pencil and you'll get the idea). Instead, much of the work is done with a tiny, pointed instrument called an ultrasonic surgical aspirator (USA), which acts like a miniature vacuum cleaner. The ultrasonic part sends tiny sound waves into the brain that destroy small sections of cells. Then the aspirator sucks these cells up and out of the head.

There are many types of brain surgery. Some surgeries that are performed to control epilepsy or Parkinson's disease involve inserting electrodes or wires into the brain. These electrodes are then attached to batteries that are placed under the skin, often near the neck or chest. The battery delivers a small current of electricity to a specific part of the brain to keep it from shutting down or going into seizures. Once the electrodes are in place, the patient only needs to have surgery to replace the battery every few years.

Another important kind of brain surgery doesn't involve opening up a patient's skull at all. It treats brain injuries and disorders by aiming tiny beams of radiation at the problem areas. Radiation is energy emitted by certain materials (metals and minerals such as plutonium and cobalt) when they are stimulated, usually by electricity. The radiation is delivered by a device called a Gamma Knife, which isn't a knife at all. It is a large, helmetlike device that aims 201 beams of radiation at a specific point in the brain, and quickly destroys the area.

Most people are afraid of the idea of brain surgery, and it's true that anything involving an exposed brain can be scary. But new devices are being invented every year to make surgery safe. And remember that neurosurgeons have almost five thousand years of history from which they've been learning.

Brain surgery is just one of the ways that doctors treat the brain. Today there are other treatments, from medication to therapy, that are available to people with brain disease or brain damage. Developing newer and safer treatments for brain diseases and disorders is a priority for neurosurgeons because, as we'll see in the next chapter, there are some very unusual things that can happen to the human brain.

How can we really follow what's going on inside the brain? Even if scientists could watch a brain in action, they still wouldn't be able to see with just their eyes what was going on. The firing of synapses is too small to be seen even by the best microscopes, but certain machines can help.

EEG

When Hans Berger invented the electro-encephalograph (EEG) in the 1920s, it was a big step forward in studying how the brain worked, since it measured the electrical activity in the brain. But it couldn't look at the structure of the brain or see if anything was physically damaged.

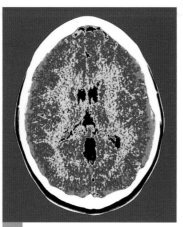

⬂ **CAT scan images are created by computers and X-rays.**

CAT

In 1972, a British electrical engineer named Godfrey Hounsfield created a machine called the computerized axial tomography scanner, or CAT scanner for short. The CAT scanner takes lots of X-rays and then fits them together into a single image on a computer. That image is called a CAT scan.

The CAT scanner looks a lot like a huge doughnut. An X-ray machine inside the doughnut circles around the patient's head, taking pictures that can be seen on a computer

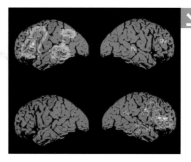

⬂ **PET scans are pictures of the brain in action.**

screen. Doctors can also view the pictures slice by slice.

Although it is composed of many pictures, a CAT scan still only shows what the brain looks like; it doesn't show anything about how a brain acts.

PET

Positron-emission tomography (PET) was invented just two years after the first CAT scanner was made. The man who created it, Michael Phelps, became interested in medicine after he cracked his skull in a car accident.

A small amount of radioactive glucose is injected into a patient's body. The radioactive glucose emits positrons, little bits of atoms that can be seen with a special camera or scanner.

The PET scan takes pictures of this glucose as it is used by the neurons in the brain (remember that the brain uses glucose and oxygen for fuel). The scan shows which parts of the brain are using a lot of glucose and a computer puts the pictures together to create images of glucose moving through the brain. These images use color to show brain activity: red for very active, blue for not very active. For instance, when a patient is talking, the sides of the brain "light up" in a PET scan. The back of the brain—where sight is processed—shows bright colors when someone is watching a movie.

MRI

Invented in 1977, magnetic resonance imaging (MRI) is used specifically to view soft tissue. It doesn't use radiation. Instead, a huge magnet moves around the inside of the doughnut. As it does, it creates a magnetic field around the patient's body. Radio waves—without the sound—are then aimed at the patient. The atoms in the body, which are now acting like tiny magnets, create their own waves when they're hit by the MRI radio waves. These waves from the patient's atoms can be measured and turned into pictures by a computer. The result is that doctors can view pictures of the soft tissue of the brain.

Functional MRI (fMRI) goes one step beyond MRI by taking pictures of blood flowing through the brain. It adds new information about brain activity because blood flow in the brain increases in those areas where the most activity occurs. So if you're raising your arm or kicking a ball, the blood level in your motor strip will be higher than some of the surrounding areas. It can do a complete scan of the brain in forty milliseconds.

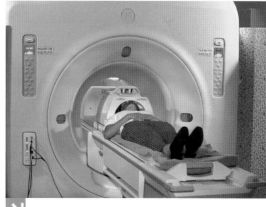

↘ **A patient lies down in an MRI machine as it takes pictures.**

MEG

Magnetoencephalography, or MEG, is a very new technology. A MEG scanner measures the natural magnetic fields in the brain that result from all of its electrical activity. It reads brain activity by using coils filled with liquid helium. These coils are cooled to almost 500 degrees below freezing—so cold that the machine's own atoms are barely moving. Since its own atoms are so still, the machine reacts to the movement of the atoms nearby—including those in your brain.

The MEG scanner is a huge and very expensive piece of medical equipment. It weighs about 8 tons—the same as four cars—and costs about two million dollars. It is by far the best way to see the brain in action, but not every hospital can afford one.

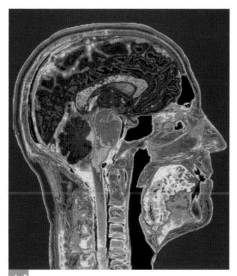

↘ **MRIs show even the softest parts of the brain.**

Treating the Brain

THe Strange Brain

Brain diseases
and mental illnesses
used to be thought
of as possession
by demons. ↗

8 THE STRANGE BRAIN

CHAPTER EIGHT

Behaviors such as shaking uncontrollably, making weird sounds, saying strange things, or having sudden spasms were once considered certain signs that the devil had entered someone's body.

Today, we know that many of these behaviors were actually caused by problems in the brain. Some of the mythical stories of people being haunted by demons are now viewed as real medical conditions that just weren't understood a thousand, a hundred, or even twenty years ago.

Because the brain is such a fragile organ, there are many things that can go wrong with it. What is amazing is that things don't go wrong very often. When the brain does break down, however, it can be deadly serious. If the brain isn't healthy, chances are that other parts of the body aren't healthy. Many of the things that we suffer from as humans, such as severe depression, anxiety, fear of flying, Alzheimer's disease, and physical ailments like Parkinson's disease or cerebral palsy can all be traced to problems in the brain.

Like other parts of your body, your brain can get sick from bacteria and viruses. These tiny organisms can occasionally break through the blood-brain barrier, causing diseases such as meningitis. Meningitis is a disease that affects the meninges, the brain's wrapping. If germs get past the meninges and infect the brain itself, it is called

The Strange Brain

ZITS INFECTED MY BRAIN

Some people think that popping pimples on your forehead will give you brain damage. While this isn't directly true—those pimples don't actually have roots in your brain or anything—open pimples can release pus into your bloodstream. And since your forehead uses some of the same blood vessels as your brain does, it's better not to have that dirty blood making its way along those blood vessels. Not that it's going to kill you, but you don't want that junk blocking up your brain's drain.

Picking your nose could also release dirt and bacteria into your bloodstream if you broke a vessel way in the back of your nose. Not a death sentence, but probably some gross habits that are best avoided.

encephalitis. Meningitis and encephalitis are rare because the brain is extremely well protected, but when these diseases occur, they are treated with medicine, as well as with rest and diet.

Other diseases start inside the brain itself. For example, brain tumors are growths in the brain that are caused by certain cells, such as glial cells, growing out of control. Scientists aren't always sure what causes this unusual growth, but it can occur due to chemicals or infection. These cells reproduce so fast that they grow to an abnormal size and start crowding out other cells. Because the cranium can't expand, these tumors might press up against neurons and cram them into tight spaces. The neurons may be crushed and even destroyed, which would affect the brain's functions. Brain tumors can be reduced by bombarding them with radiation or by removing them surgically.

One of the difficulties in dealing with brain tumors is that modern scanning devices can only show the presence and location of a tumor. They can't tell what kind of tumor it might be. In order to find out, a neurosurgeon has to go into the head and take a sample of the tumor. If the tumor is growing, it is considered to be malignant, a form of cancer. This kind of tumor can take over large sections of the brain and become fatal. If the tumor is not growing, or benign, it is still a concern because it can affect the regions of the brain around it. In both cases, a brain surgeon usually tries to remove the tumor.

Doctors can also check the health of patients who might have brain disease by making sure their cerebrospinal fluid is clear, like pure water. This is done by extracting some of the fluid from the spine in a procedure called a spinal tap. If the cerebrospinal fluid is even a little bit cloudy, which usually means it is infected, there could be something seriously wrong with the patient.

BANGING YOUR HEAD

Most of the danger to your brain comes from the outside world. It is when our heads get knocked around that our brains are most likely to be damaged. Smashing your head on the ground when you fall off a bicycle, getting hit in the head with a baseball, banging your head against a swinging door, accidentally getting hit by one of your friends—all of these are ways that your brain can get bumped around. Most of the time, your brain just swishes around inside your skull, bouncing gently off the sides. But sometimes it gets really shaken up.

If your brain is banged hard enough you might get a concussion. When someone gets a concussion, the brain is rocked around so quickly that all of its functions get jumbled. Think of it like shaking up a can of soda. Inside, everything is all fizzy and fuzzy, but after a few moments the soda in the can will settle back to its normal bubbly self. This can happen in a number of ways. It happens to athletes when they get knocked down too hard or to people who are in car accidents. Usually, a concussion doesn't do serious long-term damage, but it can "short-circuit" the brain for a few moments, meaning it shuts down some of the brain's operations for a while. People who get concussions might feel dizzy, have an extreme headache, or even lose consciousness temporarily. A concussion might even knock out a person's memory so that he or she doesn't remember what happened right before and during the injury that caused the concussion.

Interestingly, the brain itself doesn't have any feeling; it can't feel itself bouncing around inside your skull. This is because your brain has no pain receptors, or sensory nerve network. It doesn't have the kinds of nerves that feel warmth, or cold, or hardness, or softness. Each of your fingertips has thousands of these nerves—but your brain doesn't have a single one. So, you can poke it and prod it, and the brain won't feel pain. That's why early brain researchers were able to conduct tests on exposed brains—the patients they were operating on felt no pain during the tests. The researchers could stick instruments or wires into a patient's brain and it wouldn't hurt a bit.

A concussion is usually a mild brain incident. Unfortunately, there are lots of worse incidents. If a blow to the head is severe enough,

BRAIN FREEZE OR THE PAIN IN YOUR BRAIN FALLS MAINLY IN YOUR . . . MOUTH?

You've probably experienced "brain freeze" at some point in your life. That's the terrible headache you suddenly get when you drink something like a cold slushy drink really fast or eat ice cream too quickly. But even though it feels like it, brain freeze is not in your brain.

Scientists think brain freeze happens when the nerves on the roof of your mouth get shocked when the cold drink hits them. The nerves send a message to the brain saying that there's been a temperature drop in the mouth. The hypothalamus — your body's thermostat— tells the blood vessels in your head to open up, so that more warm blood can flow into the cold areas.

But as these blood vessels suddenly swell up, they put pressure on the nerves around them. Those nerves register pain and blast those pain signals throughout your head. The pain in your brain (which actually comes from the nerves on the sides of your head) is from "referred pain," which means that the pain comes from one area, but you feel it in another place.

Normal headaches are also not in your brain itself. They occur in swollen blood vessels that weave in and out of your brain, as well as in nerves and even your sinus cavities.

blood vessels can break, causing blood to leak into the brain. This is called a cerebral hemorrhage. A hemorrhage is a term that means there is a huge amount of bleeding from a broken blood vessel. When this happens anywhere, especially in the brain, it is very dangerous.

In addition to a serious smashing, another condition that can cause a cerebral hemorrhage is an aneurysm. An aneurysm is a tiny swelling on the wall of a weak blood vessel, kind of like a small bump on a balloon. If this swelling bursts, then blood spills into the brain. People who experience this "bubble bursting in the brain" can die within minutes because there is no way to repair the broken blood vessel without an immediate operation.

One of the most common injuries to the brain is a stroke, which happens primarily to older people. It's a bit like a heart attack in the head. The arteries supplying blood to the brain get so clogged that blood has trouble getting to where it needs to go. Like a blocked water pipe, the blood can't squeeze through the blockage and suddenly a part of the brain is not getting the nutrients it needs.

Stroke victims are often partially paralyzed or lose some speech ability due to the stroke. Once the stroke is cleared—usually thanks to medication called clot busters that break up the blood clot that caused it—the brain starts functioning normally again. In many cases, people who have had a stroke fully recover and regain the abilities they temporarily lost.

Blood is not the only liquid that can cause problems in the brain. Some people are born with a condition called hydrocephalus, which literally means "water on the brain." Hydrocephalus happens when the used cerebrospinal fluid in the brain won't drain back into the body. This causes a buildup of the fluid in the brain's ventricles, which makes them expand. They start to push the white matter and cortex outward and up against the skull. In babies, the pieces of the skull aren't fully locked in place, so the head may swell. The baby's head may grow to several times its normal size, like an inflated balloon.

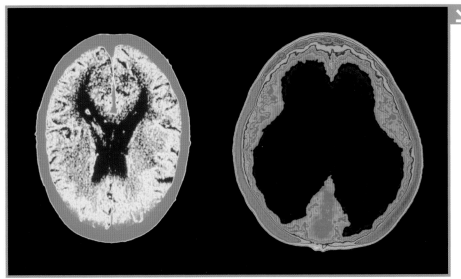

Here is a healthy brain (left) next to a hydrocephalic brain (right). Notice how much of the white matter in the hydrocephalic brain has been displaced by cerebrospinal fluid.

Hydrocephalus can result in severe brain damage, especially as the swollen ventricles push into the white matter. When this happens, white matter gets replaced with cerebrospinal fluid, and the part of the brain that should be making connections to other parts of the brain becomes flooded.

This condition is relieved by putting a tube from the baby's brain all the way down inside the body to the stomach or heart. With the tube in place, the extra fluid drains out of the brain and into the heart or stomach and then drains back into the body. If hydrocephalus is caught in time, the brain can return almost to its normal state. If not, the brain can be permanently damaged.

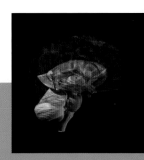

One of the most mysterious brain injuries is a coma. A coma usually occurs after a severe accident, when the brain has been both banged up and deprived of blood. Yet accidents aren't the only cause of comas. Cutting off important fuel to the brain, like oxygen or glucose, can also send a person into a coma. A person who takes too many drugs or drinks too much alcohol—which is called an overdose—can also go into a coma.

What is a coma? Basically, it's a period of time when the brain shuts down many parts of the body, almost like when you're asleep. A coma is an unusual sickness because the person *does* appear to be sleeping. But a coma is a completely different kind of

Dr. John Lorber, a pediatrician in England, discovered something truly astounding among some people who had hydrocephalus. He found that many of them, even with more than half of their brains dissolved, were perfectly normal with average IQs. In several cases, he found hydrocephalics with above-normal intelligence, including a college student who was at the top of his class in mathematics.

Lorber did brain scans of nearly six hundred patients with hydrocephalus. Some of these people were missing almost ninety-five percent of their brains! By medical standards, this meant these people had virtually no brains. He published his studies in an article that asked, "Is the brain really necessary?"

The answer, as Lorber admitted, was "yes" but it meant that some things that happen in the brain are still beyond our understanding. After all, if we think the white matter connections are so important for memory, learning, and intelligence, how could some of these people with hydrocephalus be so smart? No one knows, so we are left with yet another brain mystery. . . .

unconsciousness. Comatose patients may be aware of what is going on around them—and may actually see and hear—but might not be able to respond in any way. They may be incapable of making simple movements like blinking their eyes or wiggling their toes. They can't communicate with people in any way and appear shut off from the world.

In other kinds of comas, people have minimal brain functions and are completely separated from the world. They may not be able to hear, see, or even have real thoughts. Yet somehow their brains are keeping their bodies alive. Their brain waves show up on an EEG, but they appear to be dead.

Sometimes comas last for a few days, and sometimes they last for years. There is no known way to bring a person out of a coma. Patients just have to be cared for while they are in the coma, usually with food tubes and oxygen masks. Some people stay in a coma until they die, and some wake up one day and feel perfectly fine. We're not sure what happens to make the brain behave the way it does when it is comatose.

WHEN THE BRAIN LOSES CONTROL

It's taken many centuries, but we understand a lot more about brain diseases than we used to. In just the past few years, we've learned that a huge number of these types of problems have to do with neurotransmitters. The neurotransmitters can be blocked, misfired, misdirected, and knocked out of whack to the point where people can't control what they do.

Damage to the brain can sometimes cause epilepsy, a condition that interrupts many of the brain's normal functions. It's like having the power in your house go off for a few moments, or having the lights flicker on and off. People with certain forms of epilepsy experience wild shaking of their arms and legs, and might have all of their motor functions completely lock up. This is called a seizure. They might also black out and not even realize what has happened to them.

Epilepsy is usually treated with medication, although it may require brain surgery. One of these surgeries is known as a corpus callosotomy, which involves separating the two halves of the brain by slicing through the connections in the corpus callosum. What this does is prevent epilepsy from locking up the entire brain all at once. Since usually only one side is affected during an epileptic episode and because the corpus callosum is severed, the two sides are not communicating. The patient may remain conscious during seizures and perhaps avoid falling or having an accident. The cutting of the corpus callosum provides some relief to people with epilepsy.

Some brain conditions, including epilepsy, can be caused by genetic defects and might be present at birth. Other conditions may be the result of diseases. These include cerebral palsy, a disability in which the brain has no control over the muscles; Parkinson's disease, a neurological disease marked by rigid limbs and a shaking body; Tourette's syndrome, a disorder that is characterized by physical tics and often uncontrollable vocal sounds such as shouting and swearing; and Alzheimer's disease, a brain disease that is marked by extreme forgetfulness and eventually not knowing what is real and what is not. These conditions and diseases are never contagious—like a cold—so you can't get Alzheimer's or cerebral palsy from someone else.

Alzheimer's is a devastating disease that affects thinking. For years, when people got very old and lost their memory or started acting a little weird, others would say that they were getting senile. Now we realize that this condition is much more serious than that. Alzheimer's is a disease in which neurons and their connections break down and die, causing the brain to lose much of its memory. When the connections are gone, it is like a bridge being knocked down, and these people don't have access to even their long-term memories. They might not recognize their children, their brothers and sisters, or spouses. To make matters worse, the disease also can affect sight, speech, and movement.

Tourette's syndrome is one of the strangest disorders that occurs in the brain. It was most often associated with "crazy" people in the

SPLITTING THE CORPUS CALLOSUM

Splitting the corpus callosum is one way to treat some severe forms of epilepsy. While this operation can help the sufferer, it can produce strange and interesting aftereffects. Because the patients have their left brains and right brains separated, the two sides can't communicate.

For example, a patient who had his corpus callosum severed was shown a ball. When his left eye was covered and he was asked what he saw, the patient answered, "A ball." The uncovered right eye sent its signals directly to the left brain, and then just moved the information over to the speech center, which is also on the left side.

Next, the right eye was covered. Even though he saw the ball, he couldn't identify or even describe it because the uncovered left eye sent its images to the right side of the brain—which has no speech center. And because the corpus callosum was split, there was no way for the right brain to send the information about the ball over to the left brain's speech center.

Patients with split corpus callosums adjust to the world by making adjustments to the way they look at things. They might tilt or turn their heads in different directions so both their right and left eyes take in the same information.

past. People with Tourette's are born with the disorder, and will often make sudden jerking movements, twitch frequently, grunt or make strange sounds—all without being able to control it. Describing someone with this condition might make you think of a bag lady or a crazy person who shuffles down the streets. But in reality, Tourette's is another condition where the neurotransmitters aren't doing their jobs; they're misfiring in both the motor and speech centers. Some historians believe that the famous composer Wolfgang Amadeus Mozart and the great writer Samuel Johnson may have suffered from Tourette's. Although some sufferers may make strange physical movements or constantly twitch, their thinking brains can be working just as normally as everyone else's.

There are a few famous examples of people who developed brain disorders that affected their bodies but not their thinking. The actor Michael J. Fox found out he had Parkinson's as a young man in his thirties. Parkinson's is a disease that prevents people from controlling the movements of their arms and legs the way they want to. It is caused by the breakdown of cells in the midbrain that create dopamine, a neurotransmitter that helps keep the body moving smoothly. Without these neurotransmitters, the brain loses control over making the body move the way it should. But Fox hasn't let this disease stop him. He continues to act and is well known as the voice of Stuart Little. Because so many people know him, he has helped raise awareness about Parkinson's, and has set up a research organization to help find treatments for the disease.

Stephen Hawking, a scientist considered to be one of the smartest people on the planet, suffers from amyotrophic lateral sclerosis (ALS). This disease is also called Lou Gehrig's disease because a famous New York Yankee baseball player named Lou Gehrig had it many years ago. ALS destroys neurons that control movement, so muscles don't receive the proper commands to move. (It is almost the opposite of Parkinson's in this way.) The muscles then get weak and can't be used. People with ALS eventually are unable to move, talk, or even swallow. Hawking, a genius who has thought up incredibly important ideas about how the universe began, is confined to a wheelchair and speaks through a computer device. Even though he can't control the way his body moves, Hawking's thinking brain still turns out amazing ideas year after year.

Another unusual and barely understood brain malfunction is narcolepsy. This is a condition in which people suddenly and dramatically fall asleep for no apparent reason. They may be having a conversation, eating dinner, walking down the street, or driving a car when an attack occurs. Suddenly, they drop off to sleep. This can be very dangerous, especially if someone is driving. While little is known about narcolepsy, scientists think that both the pons and the hypothalamus are involved. They may be sending the wrong signals to the body, telling it to shut down—or go to sleep—right away. And of course, those signals are sent by neurotransmitters. In the case of narcolepsy, it may be all the wrong neurotransmitters.

NEUROTRANSMISSION AND TREATMENT

Neurotransmitters—too many, too few, or simply the wrong ones—may be the cause of conditions such as depression or anxiety. In the past, it was common to say "Snap out of it" or "Get over it" to a frequently sad, angry, or nervous person. Most people believed moods were something you could control simply by thinking them away or by changing your behavior: "Think happy and you'll be happy." While that advice can certainly be helpful in some cases, a significant number of people in the world are depressed or anxious because of neurotransmitter problems. Their depression or anxiety may be caused by a lack of serotonin, and it's a condition they cannot control.

Science has created some important medicines to restore serotonin to its proper levels in the brain. There are also drugs designed to work on specific neurotransmitters. These medicines treat specific brain conditions by affecting our neurotransmitters and keeping them in the right balance so that the brain functions normally. They seep past the blood-brain barrier to work directly on the neurons.

The Strange Brain

↘ SAVANTS

While the brain sometimes acts in weird ways we can't understand, there are other times when it does things that are truly astonishing. We don't understand these, either. There is a group of people known as "savants" who have amazing brain abilities. They usually suffer from some kind of brain damage. Some of their skills are weakened, but other skills seem almost superhuman. Many of them also have autism, which is a condition that makes it difficult for a person to develop communications skills, show emotions, or interact with other people.

An example of a savant is a young boy named Steven who was treated by Dr. Oliver Sacks, a famous neurologist. This boy suffered from epilepsy and autism. Some doctors thought that Steven was retarded. But by the age of six, Steven could draw pictures of palaces and cathedrals and bridges in perfect detail after looking at them only once. He could take a quick look at a picture of a city and then draw every building in the city. His drawings were as good as those of skilled architects, and his memory was beyond what most people could ever imagine. But Steven was never able to communicate comfortably with other people using speech.

Some savants may not be able to talk in complete sentences, but they can do math problems that usually only computers can handle. Dr. Sacks treated twins who could tell him what day of the week any date in history fell on without looking at a calendar—even moving holidays like Easter and Hanukkah. The twins could also describe what the weather was like on every day of their lives, and could count out the number pi to 300 places. But they couldn't do simple addition and subtraction.

One of the most amazing savants is a man from Wisconsin named Leslie Lemke. He was born blind, mentally retarded, and had cerebral palsy. He was also uncommunicative, and this

3.14159265358979323846264338327950288419716939937510582097494459230781640628620899862803482534211706798214808651328306647093844609550582231725359408128411174502841027019385211055596446229489549303819644288109756659334461284756482337867831652712019091456485669234603486104543266482133936072602491412 73

↘ **This is the value of pi written out to 300 places.**

made it difficult to care for him as a child. But his mother taught him how to speak and how to play simple songs on the piano.

One night, Leslie and his mother heard a piano concerto on a TV show. This was a long and difficult piano piece written by the great piano composer Tchaikovsky. In the middle of the night, Leslie's mother heard the concerto again, and thought that the concert was playing again on TV. When she got up to turn off the TV, she found Leslie at the piano, playing the concerto perfectly. She couldn't believe it. Then, she had him listen to other songs. After hearing them only once, he could play the songs perfectly. It turned out that Leslie could play anything he heard, no matter how complicated it was.

Today, Leslie performs concerts where people will request that he play songs they like. This is never a problem for Leslie; he has thousands of songs stored in his memory.

No one is sure how savants' brains work, but some researchers believe that certain areas of the brain compensate for the weakness in other parts. Other researchers think that savants might be able to focus on details in their thinking and memory because they aren't concerned about emotions or the objects or people around them. Their brains may use all their power to concentrate on things like numbers, art, or music—leaving little brain power for emotions or understanding.

The Strange Brain

Unfortunately, we can damage our neurotransmitters through the improper use of drugs. This is because individual drugs have specific effects on different parts of the brain. Many drugs increase the levels of dopamine in our brains, which make us feel good or light-headed for brief periods of time. But the more these drugs are used, the more used to the feeling the neurotransmitters become. Eventually, the neurotransmitters and the rest of our body expect that the feeling created by drugs is normal. The only way to keep the exact same feeling going all the time is to keep taking drugs. This is one of the ways that people get addicted to dangerous drugs and alcohol.

These drugs, including alcohol, create an imbalance in neurotransmitters, either activating too many or preventing others from activation at all. This can severely affect the way the brain and body work. For instance, the reticular formation may be unable to sort out all the different stimuli coming into the body, and suddenly the brain is getting too much information. This can result in the person having trouble concentrating or focusing—or even cause feelings of disorientation. Drugs such as alcohol can actually make the brain feel good, while at the same time the alcohol is eating away at the body. While the brain might crave some of the effects of alcohol for itself, alcohol abuse can destroy the liver, the stomach, the kidneys, and even the heart. Drugs like this make the brain "selfish." It stops caring about how the rest of the body is doing as long as its neurotransmitters are feeling good.

Drugs aren't the only chemicals that affect neurotransmitters. Neurotoxins do, too, and they are some of the most dangerous poisons in the world. They stop the synapses from firing and prevent them from making connections from neuron to neuron. Many neurotoxins are created by animals that use them as protection against predators. If an animal tried to eat one of these neurotoxic creatures, it would die a painful death. Producers of these neurotoxins include the poison dart frog and the bird-wing butterfly. There are also animals that use neurotoxins as a way to catch their meals. They sting or bite their prey and then

PUFFER FISH

One of the most dangerous neurotoxins is found in the puffer fish. It is a substance called tetrodotoxin, which is one of the strongest poisons on earth. This poison keeps predators from attacking and eating the puffer fish. Strangely enough, the puffer fish is considered a delicacy in Japan, where people pay a lot of money to eat it in restaurants. Chefs that serve puffer fish have to be specially trained to remove the parts of the fish's body that contain the neurotoxin. Sometimes, the chefs don't get all the neurotoxin out and sometimes, a person eats it . . . and that can be deadly.

The tetrodotoxin attacks the nervous system in the person's body, preventing neurons from communicating with one another and with the brain. Suddenly, the person becomes paralyzed. All the motor functions, along with autonomic functions such as breathing, shut down. Unless the victim is treated immediately, he or she will die. Nearly one hundred people die each year from eating expensive meals of puffer fish.

Ordinarily, fish is considered "brain food" because it contains proteins that are good for a healthy brain. The puffer fish is a major exception.

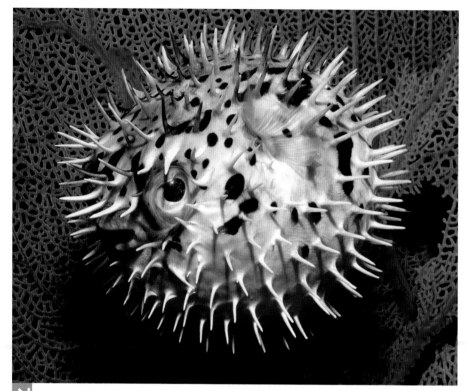

The puffer fish, also called fugu, is one of the most delicious—and deadly—fish on earth.

inject the poison into them. These animals include sea snakes, scorpions, and the black widow spider.

There are some things the brain does that we can't yet explain. We don't understand why they happen, and they are so unusual we don't know how to treat them. When we read about them or see them, we still can't make sense of them. These strange things contribute to the brain's ongoing mystery.

Dr. Oliver Sacks, a renowned neurologist, has spent his career treating patients with very strange brain ailments. He has written many books about his patients, most notably a book called *The Man Who Mistook His Wife for a Hat*. The title story is about a man who could no longer correctly identify objects that he observed. He would look at a glove and describe its shape, but he would have no idea what it was or what it was used for. He confused a parking meter with a child standing on a sidewalk. And, most interestingly, he did mistake his wife for a hat.

Dr. Sacks has seen many patients with seemingly impossible-to-understand sicknesses: a woman who heard music in her head all night long, as if her brain couldn't stop the memory function for music; a man with no long-term memory, who couldn't remember a person he had met a few moments before; an artist, who lost the ability to see colors after a car accident; and many more. All of these strange cases tell us just how much we still have to learn about the brain.

THE FUTURE OF THE BRAIN

Every day, scientists get a better understanding of what our brain does and how it works. Yet many mysteries and possibilities remain. ↗

9 THE FUTURE OF THE BRAIN

CHAPTER NINE

Will scientists one day be able to change our brains and make us smarter? Will our brains become part human tissue and part machine? Will we ever have switchable brains? These are some of the questions that scientists very much want to answer.

Scientists have learned how to transplant organs such as the heart, lungs, kidneys, and even hands. So perhaps the brain will be next. And researchers are already working on controlling animals with small computer chips implanted in their brains.

BRAIN TRANSPLANTS

Before you decide that this is all science fiction, here's something to think about: A brain transplant has already been done on a monkey. Actually, it was a whole head transplant, but the purpose was to prove that a brain could live in a new body. In 1970, Dr. Robert White, a neurosurgeon at Case Western Reserve University in Cleveland, Ohio, took the head of one monkey and surgically attached it to another monkey. When the monkey with the new head and brain woke up after the surgery, it tried to bite the finger of one of the doctors. It seemed to be quite healthy and lived for eight days.

Recently, Dr. White said that technology has advanced so quickly that he believes that human brain transplants could be possible

The Future

by the year 2050. But he envisions that brain transplants will be more like body transplants. He imagines a healthy brain, perhaps in someone who is paralyzed, being given a new body. This new body would come from someone who is brain-dead. Knowing that people might think of Frankenstein's monster, Dr. White points out that people thought heart transplants were a horrible idea when they were first performed. Now they are accepted and are done all the time.

But what will happen to a person who has a new brain, or a brain that has a new body? The brain would probably have the same thoughts it always did, but it would be in a new and unfamiliar body that had lived through events and circumstances that the brain had never experienced. Would the brain have to learn how to operate a new body from scratch, like a newborn baby's brain does? After all, this body used to receive commands from a different brain. With a new brain, it would have a new master controller. How would the body respond?

And what about putting a female brain in a male body, or vice versa? Obviously, there are many physical things that are different between a male and a female. Could a male brain adapt to a female way of existing in the world? That's something we can only guess at right now.

⬊ THINKING MACHINES

The idea of Frankenstein brings up the fact that humans have always wanted to create "intelligent" life. That means developing something in a laboratory that has a brain and can think. There are many myths and stories about humans trying to create a "thinking creature" or a "thinking machine." Some of these stories are thousands of years old and have been around ever since humans started telling stories and building machines.

It wasn't until the first computers were built in the 1940s that a machine could actually do things that resembled human thinking. Early computers were used for performing large math calculations

Who has the right
answer? The human
or the machine?

and for creating coded messages during World War II. After the war, Alan Turing, a British mathematician and college professor who worked with computers, wondered what would happen if these machines were programmed to think.

Turing came up with guidelines to determine if a computer was indeed thinking like a human. It was a game, really, called the Turing Test. Here's how it works: Pretend a human and a machine are hidden behind a curtain. A man sitting in front of the curtain asks questions to the human and the machine. He gets answers back on a printed piece of paper, but he doesn't know whether the answer came from the human or the machine. When a computer is able to answer every question so that the man thinks every answer is coming from the human, then the computer will be considered intelligent.

For many years, computer scientists have been trying to create machines that think by using a technology called artificial

The Future

Delgado also implanted electrodes in monkeys' brains.

The idea of using electricity to connect the brain to the outside world is not new. In the 1960s, a scientist named Jose Delgado inserted a small radio-controlled electrode into a bull's brain. Delgado then went out to face the bull, much like a matador in a bullfight. The only protection he had was his radio transmitter. The bull charged at him, but Delgado didn't move. Just as the bull was ready to gore Delgado, he flipped a switch on his transmitter. Suddenly, the bull skidded to a halt right in front of him.

Delgado knew the bull would stop. He had put the electrode in an area of the bull's brain that controlled how aggressive or how peaceful the bull would be. When Delgado's transmitter activated the electrode, it shut down the aggressive part of the animal's brain. The bull no longer had any interest in attacking him.

Delgado upset other scientists when he suggested that maybe people were ready for these electrode implants. He said that people who were dangerous, such as violent criminals, could be controlled using his methods. His fellow researchers didn't like the idea of putting electrodes in people's heads and then making them behave a certain way by flipping switches.

But as we've seen over the history of brain research, some ideas won't go away. Researchers at the State University of New York Downstate Medical Center have inserted electrical probes into the brains of rats. Using commands typed into a computer, they could control the rats' movements from almost a quarter of a mile away. This was much more important than just being able to stop a bull. The computer instructed the rats to move in a particular direction by sending signals that stimulated parts of their brains. Scientists think these "robo-rats" could be used to search and sniff for explosives, or even be used to find injured people in such dangerous places as war zones or earthquake rubble.

Bulls and rats are not humans, of course. There are serious concerns about how devices like these might affect the workings of the human brain. We don't want to control people with computer chips or make them do things they don't want to do.

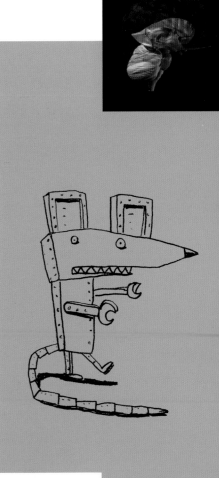

But certain kinds of computer chips for the brain are already being used to help people. Chips and electrodes are implanted in the brain to help control epilepsy. Other chips are being created to help bridge the gap between nerves that have been cut or damaged. This may allow people who are paralyzed to use their limbs again. One day sight may be restored to blind people by using a chip that processes light and sends the information along the optic nerve into the brain.

These kinds of chips may help repair and redirect nerve impulses for certain parts of the body. But what about a chip that actually makes us smarter or helps us think faster? How would this kind of brain implant work? No one is really sure. Science fiction writers have speculated that maybe the chips would contain certain information—like whole encyclopedias or instructions on how to fly a helicopter—and send it to the brain via wires hooked up to the learning and memory centers. These wires might mimic the firing

The Future

of neurons to create whole new memories and thoughts all at once in your cortex.

The idea of chip implants, the search for artificial intelligence, and the creation of a computer–brain connection are all very intriguing, and in some ways, very exciting. This research shows us time and again that the more we learn about the brain, the more we learn how little we really know. Our brains still hold more secrets than black holes or the rings around Saturn. And the questions keep coming: How are we supposed to create a machine that thinks when we're not quite sure how our own brains think? How can we upload learning instructions into our heads when we're not sure where our individual memories are stored, or how we retrieve them?

There is so much more to learn. We've been examining the brain for thousands and thousands of years, but it's only in the last few years that we've begun to uncover its most spectacular secrets. The biggest questions—such as how everything really works inside our brain, with neurotransmitters exploding around those billions of neurons—still remain. Studying the brain will continue to be like investigating a mystery, where every little clue gets us one step closer to finding the answers, and every little clue brings up more questions.

And maybe, just maybe, it will be your brain that solves the mystery of that thing inside our heads.

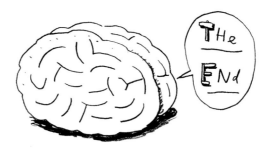

AUTHOR'S NOTE

I first remember getting interested in the brain in grade school. I had to do a science project on one part of the human body. I chose the brain because it seemed to be the most colorful and interesting part. My dad and I spent an entire evening making a life-size brain out of Play-Doh. By the time we were done piecing the different colors together, that brain was one of the coolest things I'd ever made.

After that, I read a lot of books about the brain—or activities that involved using your brain. My favorite book was *The Thinking Machine*, which is about a scientist who solved mysteries by figuring them out with his brain. Later, I found the same enjoyment reading the stories about Sherlock Holmes, who seemed able to accomplish anything and solve any mystery just by thinking clearly and logically.

When I graduated from college, I became a writer. I wrote about a lot of things—music, science, business, and medicine. But I wrote mostly about a technology called artificial intelligence. Known as AI, artificial intelligence is the attempt to make machines think and act just like people. Writing about the technology required that I learn how computers worked, and I had to understand what made computers so different from people. Because AI was such a new technology, I was one of the only people in the world writing about it for a while.

I then wrote a book called *The Brain Makers*, which was the true story of how people have tried to create brains—or thinking machines—almost since the beginning of history. Writing *The Brain Makers* made me wonder more and more about how our own brains worked. Around this time, my daughters were born, and I was amazed at how quickly they learned—faster than computers—which made me even more curious about exactly what the human brain is and how it does the things it does.

Author's Note

I started studying the brain, even reading college textbooks to learn what I could about neuroscience. It was like going back to school, except that I was my own teacher (which I think is a very cool thing). I got so interested that I started writing a fiction novel about the brain.

Then a series of coincidences occurred that led to this book. When I mentioned my brain novel to my friends at Scholastic, they told me they were thinking about publishing a science book about the brain. Would I be interested in writing it? they asked. My answer was an immediate "Yes." I knew it would be the perfect book to tie in with what I had learned.

One day, after I had started writing this book, my neighbor asked me what I was working on. When I told her I was writing a book on the brain, she told me that her father was a neurosurgeon—and he was coming to visit her that week. Would I like to meet with him? she asked. Again, I answered "Yes."

That's how I met Dr. Mike McWhorter. Dr. McWhorter has been a neurosurgeon in Winston-Salem, North Carolina, for twenty years. He has operated on the brain and the nervous system so many times, it's hard to even imagine—he's performed several thousand neurological procedures. He's also been a professor as well as the president of the Congress of Neurological Surgeons. I don't think I could have met up with a better neurosurgeon—and it was completely by chance. Dr. McWhorter spent a lot of time teaching me about the different areas of the brain that I hadn't figured out from textbooks, and then he made me an offer I couldn't refuse. He invited me to North Carolina to join him in the operating room while he and his fellow doctors performed neurosurgery. It was one of the most incredible experiences of my life.

The result of all my years of curiosity, research, and coincidence is this book. I'm glad you've chosen to read it. And I hope you have the opportunity in your lifetime to work on something that you, too, find as exciting as I find the brain.

↘ RESOURCES

There are many Internet sites and public libraries that provided me with much needed information in the middle of the day and the middle of the night. Some of them are listed here. There is no end to the astounding things you can find if you set your mind to it—look hard enough and you'll find the entire world is waiting for you.

Neuroscience for Kids
http://faculty.washington.edu/chudler/neurok.html

How Your Brain Works
http://science.howstuffworks.com/brain.htm

Neuroanatomy on the Web

Lessons from California State University
http://www.csuchico.edu/~pmccaff/index.html

The Amazing Brain
http://www.brainsource.com

The Secret Life of the Brain
http://www.pbs.org/wnet/brain/3d/index.html

Comparative Mammalian Brain Collections
http://www.brainmuseum.org/index.html

Virtual Hospital: Dissections of the Real Brain
http://www.vh.org/adult/provider/anatomy/BrainAnatomy/BrainAnatomy.html

Probe the Brain
http://www.pbs.org/wgbh/aso/tryit/brain/

Brain: The World Inside Your Head
http://www.pfizer.com/brain/

Optical Illusions
http://members.lycos.co.uk/brisray/optill/oind.htm

Interactive Stroop Effect Experiment
http://faculty.washington.edu/chudler/java/ready.html

⬂ INDEX